Surviving the Enemy

*A P*owerful *T*ruth *o*f *O*vercoming *t*he *E*nemy

Surviving the Enemy

By JB Daughter of the King

I *Dedicate This Unconditional Truth to All People Unaware of Who God Truly is in Your Life & Darkest Hour. Thank-you Lord, For Amid the Enemies' Wrath on My Life & Flesh You Covered Me. If It Had Not Been for The Love & Grace of Our God, You Whom Holds This Truth in Your Hands Would Not Have the Honor of Reading Gods Hand in My Life, & Still Covers Me Today. Nor Would I Have the Honor of Sharing My Testimonies of Surviving Countless Attacks of The Enemy. To My Beautiful Mother & Father Whom I've Lost Along the Way. Thank you, for Even During Your Battles with Cancer You Told Me to Keep Fighting.*

To My Enemy I Forgive You

Forgiveness is a gift, and if ever given it means someone out there in the world has let go of wrath.

CONTENTS

Introduction – Let God Lead   *VII*
A Letter to My Attorney (Jackie Cadman) Change Is Power!
Freudian Prince Against the Forces of Evil for My Freedom
Jesus Has the Last Say Over His Anointed! Jesus

Chapter 1.   *1*
Who Is the Enemy?
What Does the Enemy Want?   *Why Is the Enemy After Me?*

Chapter 2.   *18*
How to Defeat the Enemy
How to Kill the Enemy
How Not to Destroy Yourself Fighting the Enemy!!!!

Chapter 3.   *30*
How to Protect Your Family from The Enemy During Spiritual Warfare
How to Protect Your Psychologically Thinking from the Enemy
How to Protect Your Job and Home from The Enemy

Chapter 4.   *43*
What Do You Need to Survive the Enemy?
When Will the Enemy Attack?   *Who Will the Enemy Attack?*
Where Will the Enemy Attack

Chapter 5.   *54*
Steadfast with The Enemy
Leave Your Mark on The Enemy
Faith Leads Us to Do Only What God Can Understand

Chapter 6.   *80*
Pray for The Enemy "That's Right" Pray for them   *What Does It Really Take to Forgive the Enemy?*
Hatred Vs. Heart

Chapter 7.   *93*
Why Give God the Glory
Victory Already Written in God Promises (Jesus)
What Does it Mean to Leave the Battle to God?

CONTENTS

Chapter 8   *103*
   How You A Single Human Being Can Save Just One Person
   Kindness Without Strings Attached
   How to be A Part of Something Bigger Than Yourself

Chapter 9.   *115*
   People God Don't Know How Not to Fight for His Children
   When God Waits on You (WOW)
   Your Birth Right

Chapter 10   *124*
   My Real Father (Finally)

Introduction

How Can We Set the Objectivity If We Don't Have A Clue Where We're Going?

One's life is theirs to do as they please! At least, that's what you think until everything in your life comes to a yielding halt by forces beyond understanding. In the human quality of life, we speak greatly of what moves us, attracts us, and yet, no one speaks of the existence of detours that takes us under. There's a battle lost every day amongst each other. A regret every minute, of every second of every day. There are forces beyond our epistemology rendering us loss, lost and vulnerable to the unknown. Too often one is led with emotions vast and destructible. The good news is, our Lord and Savior is amongst us, to lead us in the right direction. You are already an overcomer of all things meant to stop, delay, and destroy you.

It Will Be You & God Conquering the Multitude of What Comes Up Against You!

With God Leading' You Will Leave an Impact in This World. So Just Let God Lead you!

Jackie Cadman

A Court Appointed Attorney & God Send Against My Persecutions

As I think back awaiting persecution from every end of the judicial system, I remember feeling like I was dying inside. The representation prior didn't think I was worth the ink and paper to build a case. I never met such an individual that could look in one's face and determine their entire humanity without facts. After appearing in front of numerous Judges, there was only one that called me to her bench, and asked me, "do you want a new attorney?" In such a dire situation, that statement sounded like milk and honey. I oblige quickly! One of the best decisions I've ever made from an offering. There's A law, "if you don't like your attorney replace them" as quick as possible." There was no mistake in the season that forged you to represent me. When I first met you, I was genuinely moved by your poise. You looked me in the eyes beyond my mess and questioned my soul. There was no sense of peace from the time I entered DC Jail, until my heavy eyes met you. From one side of the bars you looked at me, as if you already knew my story. I finally figured it out. You weren't sent to represent me, you were sent to rescue me from myself, and the evil I've encountered. From one natural ability to another, there are only a few talented works of art in this world. You Jackie Cadman are one of the mighty, chosen to lead forces beyond the human capacity. They sent me the best, of the best, in a storm brewing around my flesh. On your desk my case set upon your return from the **Thanksgiving Holiday.** Your many visits to DC Jail left gravity feeling your weight. Your appeal to my nativity right, I let this world ravage like it was prey. Trusting others over my birth right to sum up the equation. The unexplainable discovery in my case, exposed fears, power, and authority.

You knew what I was up against. You didn't hold my hand, and for sure, you didn't abandon me upon first sight. The moments of revelation, and the power of God working without knowledge. My phone call to you from **Home** learning of my release. The aspiration that stood between grace and all odds. It leveled the balance between good and evil giving me a fighting chance. My constant forge between logic and sheer determination inspired accountability, and responsibility over choices that ruled and reign over the outcome of my case. You learned who I was and tested who I wasn't in a situation that offered only scapegoating, and pure cowardice. Thus far, in an ocean I drunkenly plunged, I didn't want an easy way out from a sobered truth. I wanted an unwavering change to make no mistake of who God is in my life, situations, family, and fears. I've discovered in this impeccable challenge in my life, an occurrence appearing every few years. Almost like a movie I've grown tired of playing over, and over again. Someone once said, "you don't have to wear that same old outfit anymore" it was time for me to change the role I was playing in the enemy's game.

A much deeper change: I knew was going to take me through the trenches of my adversaries, even after my case was closed. How grave of importance you became in my life at that very moment in time. There was a power unspoken and forbidden to claim on either side. Was I guilty of what I been accused? "shooting my husband, his son, and his friend" *No!* Did the world stand still that night? ***It absolutely did!*** Could science explain it? Only the hole that appeared in my storm door. The rest I could not, not in the human terminology of explanations. Waiting, un-anticipating the statistics to choose sides, it seemed time stood still yet again. So, we waited, and waited, and waited, as all things must come to an end for new stages to begin. So, they piled up felonies to intimidate me, without physical evidence, but hearsay and probable cause. The news was astounding, as it was daring and audacious.

You looked at me and said, "let's prepare, we'll fight it to the very end." Intimidations just got bigger than my case. They wanted to break me. What the enemy didn't realize' in my weaken state, strength own a permanent place in me. It was stronger than my physical being holding me together. *No one knew this, but you, me, the gifted, and God.* Even when there looked to be a clearing, you delivered even worsen news. *News that I had been indicted.* Yet again, with me to the end you said, "let's prepare and wait." You *Jackie Cadman* are no ordinary attorney! You care about those you come to represent, fight for, defend, and pursue justice to the very end. God sent me a champion to defend my wounds and the works against me. They even threw salt to ensure I knew what I was up against. I'm just glad you made the decision to ride the brewing storm with me. There was humor between the hits. Laughter never felt so good during those iffy moments. They were dosages to lighten up, as things wasn't as bad as the physical matter deemed.

*Make no mistake, "my charges were no laughing matter" and God sent me a champion well prized in the mythology of war. I was almost sure **you** were being tested as well. I then learned you led a fleet of attorneys. God don't make mistakes, and you* **Jackie Cadman** *are no laughing matter.*

Something happened, I never imagine I would ever experience in my breathing life! I couldn't believe it was happening to me! I was disowned by my family, betrayed by my husband, and made target of every attribute in my life. The enemy then went after my daughter while I had a box on my ankle defiling her, because I wouldn't break nor plead. I had to find a way to protect my daughter, and fight both our cases at the same time. I recall saying, if that's the switch their looking for in me, then they can get it screwing with my daughter.

Everything got real in mellow seconds, ***but you***, you looked at me and knew, you just knew keeping my wits while they were hitting below the belt was only food for the surgery ahead.

Thankyou!

Even though I knew you were just doing your job, you became my defender, my family, a sister, a friend, and my light in a dark trial. I never had someone, so honest with me, that it penetrated the only thing I had left. My faith in the unknown. There was never any good news to deliver, you taught me that good can come out of a bad ending. ***Change*** could come out of a bad situations. Every which way I turned it was bad. It got so bad, I heard you say, "I'm not jeopardizing my career for you" and I said, ***"I would never ask you to do that."***

The simple awareness of such a thought to have crossed your mind, alerted me I had the right person by my side. I looked to the floor in your office and said we will find another way. You help me carry a weight, not even the village I belong was willing to help me carry. I did the only thing I knew how, and that was to pray. Every call for negotiation was to crush me still, I said "no deal." So, we walked away. One-week later felony's turned into misdemeanors, and I said, "no deal." Another week later, you looked at me and said, "what do you want to do" no deal, and we walked away. On the third week their offer seemed something that should've been offered from the very beginning, but there was a deeper meaning to a cycle that kept repeating itself in my life. A cycle that kept taking me under. A cycle that finally made sense that needed to change. This was a pattern happening in my life before you came to represent me, and before it was my time to face a challenge that plagued my bloodline before my birth. *Jackie,* it was deeper than me, but God chose me to put an end to a cycle that reign before my arrival on earth. This rare occurrence seems to happen every four years, I recognized it was bigger than me and needed to end with me.

I'm winding down to the revelation revealed during my case. There was no physical evidence revealed in my case. Not even a witness to testify against me to present at trial. This was a door opener for me to plead not guilty, as I didn't do what I was accused, but was guilty of being a drunkard. Everything I've prayed for was in front of me, and yet instead of not guilty, I pleaded. *Stay with me,* the revelation was the pattern, and cycles that kept coming for me. This was a cycle I figured in my past life I kept running from. Right there in that very moment I started making decisions for those that were coming behind me. I didn't want this stigmatization to follow me in my next life. What was happening appeared like Déjà vu and became all to coincidental to me. This was the work of the devil, and the only way to defeat this cycle was to take responsibility for my ancestors past life, or mine. Someone left unfinished business and I had to end it. End it spiritually, and physically.

This was bigger than my walking life, and it would've only gotten bigger for my daughter and the bloodline behind me. I didn't lose my case *Jackie:* I was awakened by a power I didn't know I bestowed within me. I was freed from the grips of the enemy in my past life and stood a better chance of dealing with the enemy in my walking life than taking the easy way out. I pleaded to God to break a curse older than my life's purpose. *I used my faith to fight the physicality of this world that was coming up against my persons.* There was a victory pleading against this curse that endowed my ancestors and its attack on my life. *Sacrificing the easy way out bestowed me a wisdom stronger than what most humans will obtain in this life.* The endurance of accepting a responsibility of battling forces too insane to discuss, left me feeling perplexed and asking why my ancestors didn't finished this battle before my walkabout on this earth.

My ancestors did their part *Jackie*, as yours, endowed before you. It was meant for our paths to cross in this life. There was a battle before our acquaintance, and whatever the past life battle pertained, there was no doubt favor was given over the enemy. All religion makes up the body of Christ in my walking life, and I believe that same power was upheld in our past lives leaving a path for us to cross helping me once again to defeat a mutual enemy. I was taught to choose my friends wisely and to test every spirit. *We have indeed been tested!*

You *Jackie Cadman* have a friend in me. You are a person of integrity and unpersuaded to Honor and back. You can look death in the eyes and promise the dead Justice and will pursue to it to the very end. You wear empathy to a fault and still deliver. Behind closed doors you are still working for the people you represent. On you are the promises of your best!

Even when all odds are against what you represent. You *Jackie* I choose as my friend; I choose my friends and you're the realest person I've *EVER* met in my walking life. Point-blank period! You are your oath, the truth, nothing but the truth, so help you God.

You will always have Favor in me.

Until we meet again Friend. I hope under different circumstances. Lol Jesus...

JB, Daughter of the King.

CHANGE IS POWER

"I didn't know the love of our Lord and Savior until He rescued me." Several times to ensure I make no mistake it was His Grace and Mercy on my life as He found me worthy to be saved."

I met God through my molestation tribulations. He sustained me to survive all these years. At just five years old He was sustaining me to survive the molestation to tell my experiences of survival to all the little girls of the world that was once me. At the age of twelve I blew up in my mom's kitchen while doing hair. At the age of fourteen I was pushed into a moving train. At the age of sixteen something in my closet scared me terribly, and revealed to me spirits and demons were real. At the age of eighteen someone that loved me threaten to kill me at gun point. At the age of thirty-two the enemy attacked me full force. I'm short cutting on the occurrences, but each time my ancestors and guardian angels were right there with me. Each time something, or someone appeared before me informing me, in some strange occurrence not yet. ***All's*** I knew was, one day I was at the top of my life with a new job, finishing graduate school, happily married, and mother to a very beautiful young lady, and daughter to a very strong woman. Aunt to a handful of nieces and nephews. Sister, and cousin to generational bloodlines. A niece to Aunts and Uncles guarded by those in the hereafter. Yes, the hereafter is real, and they'll do whatever it takes to get your attention to let you know you're not alone.

Fight Back -Or- Die for Nothing

Everything that meant anything to me was shaken and stricken from me all on one Thanksgiving night. A day we're to give thanks and share the kindness of the Lord with others. On November 22, 2013 the Lord made sure I knew who He was, and His power over my life. He made sure I would have no reason to question the occurrence on this very Thanksgiving Day, as it was the day, He fought the forces of evil for my life in my home I couldn't believe my eyes and the supernatural that was unfolding before me. I asked myself day after day, week after week, month after month, and year after year. What made me so special that the Lord God Himself would reveal Himself, just to protect me? Protect me He did against every force that dared to threaten my being. I don't question what makes me so special. I simply use my gifts to better this world and those that need proof.

Freudian Princes Against Forces of Evil for My Freedom.

We ask, "where do our help come from" and I reveal it clearly, "look again" were not alone. I wept like a child when the Lord revealed Himself to me. I'm still astonished at the angel that stood by my side when I was pushed into the train. I still felt the heat when I blew up in my mother's kitchen but was "pulled" through the fire and survived what should've been my entire body. Convicted with confidence when my ex-pointed a gun at my face. I'm not afraid as before of the monsters in my closet. They're more afraid of me! I now know now who I am and aware of the gifts God has instilled in me before my birth.

Who am I, "I am JB Daughter of the King"

Hail King Jesus!

Jesus Has the Last Say Over His Anointed!

Be Aware of Your Purpose in this World.

This is for anyone that believes their life is over! I'm here as living proof that our God exist. If it had not been for Him on multiple occasions, I would've perished in the pit my enemies set for me many times over. *A fool's, fool can only be fooled so many times before the lesson of being a fool will ever reveal itself one has been fooled.* (Yes) Nourish that for a minute. If you find yourself feeling like déjà vu, maybe it's because you've experienced, or lived through something familiar or been here before. Don't doubt it, because you have, and you're being played as a fool. The enemy and the spirit of the enemy go, hand in hand, working together to delay you, or better yet keep you from reaching your life's purpose. If this isn't clear enough, and you're still finding yourself saying, "somethings not right" that's your heart led spirit screaming to you from the other side, the hereafter, the firmament where the throne of Jesus sits sending you a message saying *(wake up)* it isn't over yet. Don't get caught up in what's exciting and run with it, but yet take a step back and ask yourself, "what would Jesus do" we were made in His image, tempted like He was tempted and persecuted just like He was persecuted. Mathew *4:11* reads as follows, "Jesus has just rebuffed Satan's third temptation and ordered him away. The devil departed and Jesus was serviced by angels. So, I'm telling you when you're able to rebuff the likes of *déjà vu* and decern the difference between your voice, the enemies voice and Jesus voice, you will follow the voice of Jesus all your remaining days. It's never too late to get right I don't care what your mistake was!

CHAPTER ONE

Who Is the Enemy?

Don't be fooled! The enemy is anything and anybody not God sent! The enemy wishes you ill intentions set to hinder you, delay you or to stop you from being everything that God wants you to be. When you're destined for something that means, the enemy is going to gain by your loss and suffering. The enemy is put in place to distract you, and even use against you what matters most. ***The enemy is even you if you're not careful.*** The enemy is a mere reflection of the opposite of greater He is in you. The enemy is the weakness to God's strength in you. The enemy is a shortcut that deters you from the right direction. The enemy is the voice of destruction. The enemy is the cause of frustration and making hasty decisions. The enemy is the thought behind our flesh-eating ways. The enemy is the stipulation in being indecisive, and unable to come to sound decisions. The enemy is the thought of hate. The enemy is the reason before and after murder and why we choose to end the power of God that lives within us. The enemy is the reason of adultery that causes separation and renders divorce as the outcome. The enemy is the cause of families dividing property and children when love is supposed to conquer all. The enemy is the behavior of trickery and illusions we feed our souls to believe in the physical world, and not the Holy Spirit that promises us our hearts desire. The enemy is the reason of sicknesses, instead of sickness in health until death do us part. The enemy is the reason behind our negative "thought life" instead of a spirit filled life. The enemy is the reason your dreams are not realized. The enemy is the reason we seek to destroy each other and take each other out. The enemy is the reason why families dis-own their offspring's and cast them out in a world they cannot survived without the covering of the Holy Spirit. The enemy is the reason we give up without fighting. The enemy is the reason we avoid responsibility for our failures instead of learning the lesson we failed.

Fight Back -Or- Die for Nothing

The enemy is the reason we judge each other. The enemy is the reason we refuse to steadfast in Gods promise for our lives. Promise #1 God is always with me (Never Fear). Promise #2 God is always in control (I will not doubt). Promise #3 God is always Good (I will not despair). Promise #4 God is always watching (I will not falter). Promise #5 God is always Victorious (I will not give up). These are just a few promises of God. He is our strength and leads us to prosper. He hears our prayers and will answer you to let know it was Him that answered your heart's desire. He will fight for you when all else fails. He will give you peace during the storm, and He will always love you. He is the Omega, all Mighty God that keeps His promise to His Children.

Wait on Him!

Surviving the Enemy

The enemy is the reason we isolate our gifts. Everybody has a gift within them from God. The enemy is the reason we are silent and turn a blind eye to the ugliness of this world. The enemy is the reason our children repeat our mistakes. The enemy is the cause of losing our children to these streets, mayhem and chaos. The enemy is the reason our sons and daughters never become the kings and queens they're meant to be, often missing their life's purpose. The enemy is the reason our sons and daughters don't have a father to protect them. God didn't create us to be caged. He created us to multiply to fulfill His kingdom. ***Not to fill the prison system!*** The Head of His kingdom doesn't belong in jail, he must run His castle, and protects his family, while leading His sons and Daughters in the way it's imperative for them to go, while Wisdom the Women wraps her tail around the entire unit of her family keeping them all covered in the Blood of Jesus. When you have this ability of power over your family the enemy has nothing coming. ***Nothing!***

The enemy is the reason a blind eye is turned when our children are molested and grow up to be tested by our parental faults! ***King Jesus help me Selah this aggressively.*** By all exposure "We Must be Preventative." This is happening in front of the naked eye, visible eye, third eye and we do nothing. I'm here because God sustained me to tell of my survival in this testimony. You don't get to drop me off no more to the molestation. You don't get to act like you didn't know anymore. You don't get to say, "it will never happen again" and it did over, and over again. You don't get to let the molester come in anymore. ***Today God gives His children power of exposure, and that power will expose you!*** You see something, say something to protect them! You see something, save them from the perpetrators that molest in plain sight! You hear something say something to expose them.

Help Jesus Selah!

Fight Back -Or- Die for Nothing

The enemy is the reason alcohol is a mental illness but display in our physical lives as destruction. The enemy is the drinking and drugging we can't stop, because it's easier to be someone else disguising our physical faults. There's an old sane, *"A Drunken Mind Speaks A Sober Truth."* Or' is it the pain we're too fearful to tell when we're sober. The enemy is the coward hidden beneath the surface keeping us from building an unconditional relationship with God. The enemy came before us and will be here after us. The enemy is the reason we fail to trust GOD! Nowhere in any body of Christ does He tells us to trust our human counter parts, or humans. But, oh how He pleads with us to trust Him, know Him, and simply believe in His promise. The enemy knows our existence is temporary. Who is the enemy you ask me? "He is an angry angel kicked out of Heaven" and will stop at nothing to stop you and yours from reaching your appointments that God has destined for your purpose.

Surviving the Enemy

What Does the Enemy Want?

The enemy wants everything that makes you "You." He wants everything that makes you happy and whole. **OMG,** imagine giving just a little of your joy to the enemy. Imagine that! He wants to ruin the lives of those that represent God and use those that don't believe to destroy the kingdom of God. We make it *too* easy for the likes of evil! We give in *too* easy to the likes of the enemy by volunteering our weaknesses to those that come in sheep's clothing, disguise in the eyes of those we hold dear, and in the eyes of those we trust. The enemy wants everything that has been denied to *him/her* existing amongst us. The enemy wants to cause mayhem, destruction, illnesses, grief, financial lost, divorce, treachery in the home, workplace, churches, and places of covenant and peace. The enemy wants the sole of those that are predestined to be used by Christ. He wants the flesh of those untainted, and the pureness of those untouched for his own pleasures. **His own pleasures!**

The enemy wants to build an allegiance against God. He wants to use you to betray the Holy Spirit. One, in which, you've encountered if you're reading this book. The title of this book is going to draw the attention of the enemy and is going to draw the attention of shepherd's, prophets, guardians, ancestors, messengers and even Christ Himself will get a hold of the FIRST copy, as I pour out this truth, He wants you to own. The enemy wants to stop this manuscript from ever seeing the light of day. The enemy doesn't like us testifying to the victory of Christ, but only to our suffering and addictions. The enemy despises God so much it makes the enemy sick to hear us praise Him and give God all the Glory for which it belongs. The enemy wants you to feel like you don't belong. The enemy wants you to feel isolated and alone with no one to call on. Know that God will never leave you alone to call on your weakness. *That will be your flesh, not God!*

Fight Back -Or- Die for Nothing

Know that God wants you at your best. The enemy wants you to call his name. Rebuke the devil in the blood of Jesus.
Rebuke his name as the HYPE you need comes from Jesus. The enemy wants to remove that hedge of protection God has place around you since your birth. The enemy is pissed-off that God has chosen you amongst the weakest to ensure His word is kept. The enemy wants to remove every head of every household to attack the wisdom and children as the head lay headless. ***Pause!***

The enemy wants to overtake what God has destined for you and yours. This isn't just about you, it's about what you're working so hard to preserve. The enemy wants to ruin your children to keep them from carrying on the bloodline into the future. The enemy is nasty, dirty, cheap in breathing, ugly in acting, and revealing to those with the gift of discernment. The enemy needs your soul to survive, it needs your children's soul, your neighbor's souls, friends of friend's souls to survive. At our weakest moments and vulnerabilities, we give in to the likes of the enemy, because were too weak to hold on to the promise of God, but quick to be fulfilled with the physicality of this world. ***Let me say this,*** "when you leave here, you can't take none of the material world with you." It's not getting into the gates of heaven, and it's not making it through the gates of hell.

Fight Back -Or- Die for Nothing

Why Is the Enemy After You?

Before you, or I were born our destinies had already been designed for us to nourish this world and live. Our steps had already been taken in our previous lives prior to the one we live today. That's right, we've been here before, failed and succeeded in our past lives. There's that, *"déjà vu"* experience again. We have been chosen to suffer for many reasons. We've been chosen to rise like the phoenix before, and after every challenge that comes up against us. *We have been created to fail and take the big hits just for the enemy can see us get back up again, and witness, what one would call supernatural.* This is no magic trick people! You and I know it is nothing, but God Himself reminding the enemy as it states in the book of Job (1: 9), *"have you considered My Servant Job" that there is none like him on the earth, a blameless and upright man, one who fears God and shuns evil.* This is you and me blameless and upright fearing God and shunning *ALL* evil.

Those of us whom stand blameless to man and repent only to God receives His mercy and grace. God already knows those who are pure in heart. It states in the book of Mathew (5:8), "Blessed are the pure in heart, for they shall see God." *I stand before the world, and shout loud and clear seeing me is proof of our God.* Reading what I'm pouring out is proof that God is real and amongst us. It melted my heart to know He seen me as being pure in heart. *Stay with me,* "I'm testifying to a testimony not even I foresaw" it melted my heart that my King found me worthy to reveal Himself to me in my darkest hour(s) and darkest nights." As I reveal these words in black and white, it was crystal clear of how our Lord and Savior came for me, pulling me out of the pit the enemy thought I was condemned and ruin.

Surviving the Enemy

I'm testifying, to fact that "the enemy is after us because of a pattern of attacks, and events in our past lives. **Stay with me,** you were born weren't you! That means somebody had to die for you and I to be born, and live while those before us paved the way! We suffer the attacks of our ancestors and past generational curses. Amid living life, you're wondering how everything got so messy and turned upside down. *No!* This is real, it's been happening since before you were even thought about, to someone that looked like you, talked like you, believed in the same morals and values like you do. They fought the same enemy then, just like we're fighting the enemy now. I know the enemy personally, and every chance the enemy gets, that liar is going to send the cells of evil dominion out to claim what it can of your life. The enemy doesn't have nothing else better to do, but to make your life miserable as hell is hot. And if the devil himself comes for you, that means it's personal. I'm sharing my testimony to it, **stay with me**, because he came for me in the flesh. Mathew 5:11 Blessed are you when they revile and persecute you and say all kinds of evil against you falsely for My sake. When the plot of the enemy doesn't work. Watch out, as the plot will show up in person!

The Enemy Wants the God in You.

Fight! Your Ancestors Did It! You Can Too!

Fight Back -Or- Die for Nothing

Why Do You Think the Enemy After You?

What Do You Plan on Doing About Your Problem?

Surviving the Enemy

Would Jesus Approve of Your Answers?

_____

Are Your Solutions Illegal? Lol

_____
_____

Are You Going to Jail?

_____
_____

If You Answered Yes to Two of the Questions Above, You Need to Pray & Wait on Jesus.

_____
_____
_____
_____
_____
_____
_____
_____
_____
_____.

As a reminder of how quick our flesh is please review your answers as often as possible. It can save you from a trip to Jail or worse.

Thank Jesus Not Me!

Fight Back -Or- Die for Nothing

People' *listen,* I plead with you, we're so ignorant to our flesh' even during sinning God still protects us. Even, amid our flesheating ways He still protects us. He's already aware of where our destinies are going to lead us and brings us through. This was written in spiritual warfare before we existed. I'm just re-writing it to testify how the attacks of the enemy are generational. I didn't ask for this, but I certainly played a part in my past life and this one. *I ask you* "what are you going to do differently?" We were already planned and thought-out to suffer and prosper, and stop saying, *"you didn't ask to be here."* No, you didn't, but *SomeMightyBody* being *God* decided it was ok for you to be born. Being born takes a great permission, power, and *All* authority. You are not a mistake! The greats didn't just skate through here. *HOV lane my ferry.* The HOV lane is like living a God-fearing life. Don't get caught sleeping on the enemy p*eople.* The devil is a coward and the cells under him are cowards and they do cowardly things. *Period!*

I'm being modest, but I don't want to skate away from sharing my testimonies with you. God intervenes in our flesh-eating ways. He sends us warnings, or should I say some of us have gifts, and refuse to accept them, or use them for the greater good to help others. The night before I was attacked, viciously might I add! I was sent a clear warning from my assigned guardian angel that Satan was coming for me personally himself. As I mentioned earlier in the text, when the enemy comes for you personally, it's personal. I recall very vividly every detail of my dream. I laid there asleep, deep asleep, so deep that I remember every part of the dream to share my testimony to it. Some of us have dreams and can't remember by the time we awaken to take notes. Few of us remember them to the microscopic details. Why are we able to do this? Simple, there's a message that God is trying to convey for us to survive the attacks of the enemy. Lord thank you for keeping me after all the chaos!

Surviving the Enemy
The Dream/Prediction

I dreamed I was in my bed with my husband resting like any other normal night. This giant anaconda came into our room and lifted its head above the bed's length looking for me. This was no normal size snake but and anaconda. I've seen the movies anaconda with Ice Cube and Jennifer Lopez. I watch Sci-Fi with all those crazy Croc movies vs. Anacondas. No, this was real people. I awaken quickly terrified. I'd awaken my husband to share my dream. This is not the first time I had a dream, and it came true. I have helped countless people in my past by warning them with dreams I've had about them. Some people want to know, and some people don't want to know. If you knew what I knew you would want to know when the enemy is coming for you. I awaken my husband and I told him, "I just had a bad dream" that this big snake came into our bedroom looking for me.

He nodded and went back to sleep and so did I, but not well at all. People the next day "Thanksgiving Day" of 2013 was the worst day of my born life.

This chapter is about, *"why is the enemy is after you"* it should be clear by now, but *I'm* afraid this is where we go deep for a minute. *Stay with me!* The enemy is pissed-off that we keep finding ways to defeat the chaos created in our lives. Even if it's the smallest victory in Christ. Satan is very, very hateful in anything that prospers you. *Here we go just ride!* When our ancestors fought the enemy, they were already preparing the bloodline. Yours and mine, see John 15:5 I am the vine, and you are the branches. If a man remains in me and I in him, he will bear much fruit. This is true for the fruits of warfare. Someone was fighting for you before you arrived here on earth. This didn't just start when you purchased this book. Your attack was planned, and your victories were decided somewhere else.

Fight Back -Or- Die for Nothing

People, history really does repeat itself. If God decided to assign you your ancestors, guardian angels, spirit guides, shepherds to fight and protect you in the present, that means it was already a battle won. *I hope you didn't miss the prediction right here.* This means someone died and sacrificed for you to be here. For you can fight the same demons that your ancestors before you had to fight. This is about the enemy of your ancestors destroying your blood line. This is what the enemy wants from you. Satan wants to stop you from breeding. He wants to destroy your offspring to stop them from breeding within the blood line that gave them hell. Hotter than the hell from which they came. **He wants to make sure we don't multiply, and we must ensure the opposite!**

Surviving the Enemy

The enemy is here people, disguised dressed like your coworkers, neighbor, friend, sister, brother, uncle, aunt, and the enemy will even use your children against you. ***Jesus take the wheel.*** People, we have got to wake up from our own flesh- eating ways. It's deeper than what we think and came prepared for. When I say the enemy came for me in my own home, I mean it people. I mentioned earlier seeing me or reading this book is proof that God is real. I'm here because God said so. ***See, when God Himself has His hand on you, can't nobody have you.*** They can pull at your legs, ankles, feet, hair, clothes, and even tug at your soul, but if God got you by your self-eating flesh, they still can't have you. Know this' it states, in ***"2 Corinthians 10:3-6 For though we walk in the flesh, we do not war according to the flesh."*** My God, **OMG** this is what we do before we're able to acknowledge that we just gave Satan the glory that belongs to God. ***V:4*** For the weapons of our warfare are not carnal but mighty in God for pulling down strongholds, casting down arguments and every high thing that exalts itself against the knowledge of God, bringing every thought into captivity to the obedience of Christ." ***It's Ok, nourish it later.***

Some of us don't even know what obedience is? In my experience and past excuses, I call it, "due ignorance" but you can't claim it, if you've been taught what it means to be obedient. Being obedient means, "you know who the Lord is in your life." Being obedient means your parents have been taught because they taught you. If you haven't been taught you only get a pass once to the age of recognition of (due ignorance). I want you to fully understand how this applies to you, and how it hit me like a ton of bricks. ***Psalm 22:12-13*** many bulls have surrounded me; strong bulls of Bashan have encircled Me. ***V:13*** they gape at me with their mouths, Like a raging and roaring lion.

Fight Back -Or- Die for Nothing

People, this is yet another dream while in the pit I was left for dead, that came to pass of the roaring so close to my flesh, I then realized that it was God telling me, "He was very, very angry with me.*" In Job 1:10-12, let's get back to where were hanging in the clenches of God's hands by our flesh.* Jacked up is what my pastor would say. Yet again, you asked *"why is the enemy after you"* are you still wondering, well here it is again! Satan said to God about you and me, not just Job "haven't you placed a hedge of protection around them, and around their household, and all around every side of him? Satan goes on to say to God "you have blessed the work of their hands, and their possessions have increased in the land."

People ***stay with me!*** And the Lord said to Satan, "Behold, all that he has is in your power" only do not lay a hand on his person." ***People***, we experience this trauma every day, our sons and daughters are being murdered by carnal weapons, by each other with the grandstand assistance of Satan "the enemy." We're losing our homes, marriages, jobs, families, friends, and even then, were left out there to fend for ourselves in our stinking thinking we've develop when our backs are against the wall. *We*'re being attacked from all four corners by raging bulls wanting to devour our flesh. But behold in Job (1:12) God said unto Satan, "you bet not put your hands on my child."

Surviving the Enemy

We are ALL his children. Don't go another day disowning the Lord Jesus Christ! ***That's my Father period! Oh God I hope you are getting this!*** That Thanksgiving Day in 2013, and the night before I received a premonition, a warning in the form of a dream. In the dream Satan, himself came for me. I ignored the warning signs people. The battle was so great I thought I was in a movie, but it was real, and God told Satan, "not to put his hands on me." ***Pause*** the enemy *(Satan) was so greedy he couldn't help himself, and neither could God!* I witnessed Satan and God in my home in one night. Satan had his hands on me, but my God had a better grip. Let me translate this for you, *"in your past life there was victory for you."* In this life, there is an abundance of joy that awaits you, and in order to receive the glory of God' you have got to end the cycle in which you came from, generated from, and transcended from. God has a grip on you, but will allow Satan to test your flesh, because you're too busy tossing away the protection governed by our ancestors, and guardians that fought relentlessly for us to have the protection of our God given bloodlines. ***In which we're all connected.***

In one night, I lost my family, friends, career, job, husband, and ***almost lost my beautiful daughter.*** That day was not the day to give thanks to those that weren't worthy of my unconditional kindness and love. ***It was the day schedule to change my life.*** This day had already happened in spiritual warfare before I was born and battled by many of my bloodlines before me. There is nothing wrong with you. You're gifted and chosen to do the work of our God. If attacks are many, it's because your bloodline was powerful before you, and even more powerful now in this life. ***That is why the enemy is after you!*** This is why God has you by the collar of your flesh. He is saving you for a battle that's about to repeat itself in your life! ***Break the generational curses! End them!***

Fight Back -Or- Die for Nothing

Gods knows that Satan and his demonic cells wants to stop you from finishing what your ancestors, guardian angels, spirit guides have battle over, and over again in spiritual warfare since evil and good started co-existing with each other.

Satan is after you because, he wants vengeance from all he has lost in Christ. The Lord oversees everything even if he must swoop in Himself and rescue you from yourself. Still wondering why Satan is after you. I know why he came for me! *First off,* he doesn't want me finishing this book! *Second,* he knows I struggle with fertility, but God. People, Satan is after you because, he wants you to cease to exist. You see, he's already been defeated by your ancestors before you were born. *My God*, people we weren't just born yesterday. Yet you've been here before in your past life and it isn't "déjà vu" you're experiencing. The next time something feels familiar to you (STOP) and ask God, pray on it, meditate on it, ask for clarity on it, and then watch the powers that be.

CHAPTER TWO
How to Defeat the Enemy

Here's the most undisputed truth I know for my life depended on the very foundation I write this peace of mind for you. ***You cannot defeat the enemy without God leading the battle.*** You cannot defeat Satan and his cells without the Armor of God! Derived from Ephesians 6:11 states, "Put on the whole armor of God, that ye may be able to stand against the wiles of the devil." The devil is the enemy wrapped in sheep's clothing's identical to deceit, trickery, treachery, adultery, addiction you name it, I assure you it's not from God.

Our flesh tells us to kill, steal, lie, betray, trick, commit adultery, abuse our children, mistreat our spouses and families. You can't defeat the enemy with abnormal thinking. I don't care how many times you got around your sin. I care about your day coming. *Are you prepared?* It wasn't God who came for me first. It was Satan and his cells. God came afterwards. *In fact, He was right on time!* The thought had crossed my mind to just give up. In the words of the Angels God sent with clear messages. They said, to me *"not yet"* I'm going to tell you what the enemy doesn't want you to know. It's the very same thing that kept the enemy away. ***The relationship you have with God.*** When you're connect to God the enemy can't get in. It states in the book of Proverbs (1:10) "My son, if sinners entice you, do not consent. Do not consent" (V:11) If they say, "Come with us, let us lie in wait to shed blood; Let us lurk secretly for the innocent without cause." You're protected from sinning by not listening to your flesh, you do this by not waiting on "lil James" to bend the corner and then shoot him in the head, because your flesh "oh, I'm sorry your manhood has been tested." You don't have nothing to prove to your block or, the "cells of Satan" that you're ready to give your life or go to jail for. Satan has one purpose for those he recruits. One! That's to take your life rather it be by strife or jail" either way you lose. *If the block is your limitation give God a chance!*

Fight Back -Or- Die for Nothing

People, it's that easy for Satan to come into your life. He comes and goes as he pleases. My family can't come and go as they please anymore. I don't have the luxury of friends or foes anymore that can come and go and do as they please. You got to call me first. *You anything letting toxic enter in and out of your lives.* Don't be offended stop letting everybody in before they bring in tools set to destroy you from the inside out. *I don't have the luxury of milk and honey for you anymore.* This Milk and Honey reminds me of my harvest to come after sowing in the (dirt) they called me. "I will not repeat Thanksgiving Day of 2013" it's not that *"sweet"* with me anymore. Isn't that the saying in the streets "sweeter" than liquorish. *I am not.* You supposed to be warning "lil James" not taking his life then losing your life for taking "lil James" life. **Dominos.**

My God, you missed that domino effect right there. You see how this works; it's how Satan operates. You defeat the enemy by switching up the way you operate, and the way you think in wanting to seek vengeance. Thank-you for this door opener! Plain and simple vengeance belongs to God the original OG. I'll explain this (OG) complication later.

You're not ready....JB

Surviving the Enemy

You defeat the enemy by switching up the way you respond to the cells of the enemy. Know this, when you step outside your house in the morning the enemy is waiting on you. If it's not the enemy personally, the cells of the enemy are out there waiting on you. I switched up "everything" and I wanted the enemy to know it. If we we're going to do battle, "it was going to be a show down to remember." I'm talking about being prepared to make history, but that's not how our God operates. I was to bow down or get down. *I didn't do either and neither are you!* You defeat the enemy by "repenting" with a pure heart. Let me elaborate a little about this. You don't have to repent to man, your spouse, mother, friends, family nor James's killer. Get on your knees repent to God Himself and watch what happens. **Repenting** is going to make Satan angry, and guess what? You're still giving God the glory for He will see you through any consequences that should've killed you, and yet spared you. Please tell me you're nourishing this. **Hopefully.**

I have a few more pieces on this, and then I'm going to move on. It's important you get this next segment, "discerning whom the cells of Satan are will save your life, family, your job, home, your children, your children's children and even your sanity." People, I can't shout this "LOUD ENOUGH" listen to your gut instincts, annoying feelings, senses, intuition, whispers in your ear, and too hard of a wind smacking the clarity in you. People, this is where you listen to the signs of human nature and life. "Your Life" is speaking to you. Your life is crying out for you to live, steadfast, but through God. What do I mean by this! God is not saying let Craig bully you but teach Craig what's in your pocket he may not want! Warn the enemy! Let the enemy know who Lord over your life is, and share with the enemy, you once read a story in the King James Bible (KJV) about a boy name David who slayed his Giant. Yes, teach Craig nourishment. We're all yearning to learn. We just need a little help getting there. It's (willpower) if you're unaware of what you need.

Fight Back -Or- Die for Nothing

You weren't just born yesterday ***"Lord God Selah"*** help me relay this to the people. I'm so hung up on what God has done for me, it inspired me to warn you of how sly the enemy really operates in this here ***Heirloom*** you hold in your hands. This here is nourishment...

The Lord spoke very clearly to me, and I quote Him clearly "maintain and read Me" He was clear. It still astonishes me. You will make no mistake when He speaks in clear voice to you! The second experience with my Father happened after my first experience when my King rescued me. Removing me from the very pit the enemy had sent me to rot like rotten flesh. This book wasn't created to scare you stupid. Apparently, if you're reading this book it isn't Satan you need to be afraid of "it's God." ***Come on now stay with me!***

Why do you think God gave Satan permission to destroy everything we cherish and hold true? The physicality of this world belongs to our flesh-eating ways. Unconditional love belongs to Christ Jesus For He gave it to His last breath, and still empowers in us, the power of the Holy Spirit to live! We got to go through Jesus to get to God and then the Kingdom. Come on people I challenge you to try opening your heart to Jesus. ***You tried everything else.*** Now try Jesus out for size. I know He fits well in my life. I wear my Jesus piece every day, and ***no*** not the ***Holy Glock.***

Surviving the Enemy

Someone once told me I didn't have to wear that old wardrobe anymore. Meaning my old life. So, I tried out the wardrobe of Jesus. I got Jesus all over me, and I don't look like nothing I been through. I just hope the word heart isn't too soft of a word for you to tempt the taste of Jesus. **How about this then**, open your eyes and see the grace God has for you. If that's not enough to convince you, what about that feeling you get when you see God bless someone you think didn't deserve it, but God thought otherwise. Yeah, you know that *(how)* feeling, or that adrenaline pumping through your vein saying, "I hope I don't miss my blessings, because the blessings of God look good on someone else." God doesn't want you mistaking his works in your life with no one else's but Him! **Jesus help me Selah this.** Man is in the image of God himself Genesis (1:27) So, God created mankind in his own image, in the image of God he created them; male and female he created them. I love this verse, because it mentions woman as an equal to man. **My God follow this word.** Lord I'm not even going to raise the "glass ceiling" on this. **Not Yet!**

God said, "go be fruitful and multiply; fill the earth and subdue it; have dominion over the fish and the sea, over the birds of the air, and over every living thing that moves on the earth." Let me take you back just a few paragraphs. Didn't I tell you that SATAN don't want us multiplying having off springs, with the will of God in them to carry your bloodlines into the next life reaping what we've sowed here in this life. People, to defeat the enemy we must instill in our off spring's the truth of spiritual warfare. I am not telling you to go have children and don't have a pot to uphold you, nor a hole in the wall to dispose all the mess. I'm telling you to do it, **"What Way? God's Way! The Only Way!"** Your ancestor, guardian angels, spirit guides including God Himself will be very proud of your discernment during the spiritual warfare we're living in right now. **Let's finish this chapter well.** To defeat Satan, you're supposed to be able to take a hit without wanting to seek vengeance.

Fight Back -Or- Die for Nothing

Help me Selah this again King Jesus. Some of you don't even know that the Holy Spirit, Jesus Christ our Lord & Savior, the scripture being the word of God, and God are all one. I know you didn't for those of you being taught. When you retain a relationship with the Lord Jesus Christ it isn't nothing no one can do to deter you from God. That's yet another promise of King Jesus! When God calls you to act, trust me you won't hesitate.
Even in your mess you won't hesitate to act when it's your turn to respond to the will and way of God.

Period!

Selah.

Surviving the Enemy

How to Kill the Enemy (YEP)

My God, ***delicacy*** is needed here, Jesus take the wheel and guide this message without intentional fault. ***Here goes nothing.*** This is why some people are no longer amongst the living, and somewhere else. I strongly believe in a system where we live today of target or pre-target! I will break this down for whom needs it. ***Veterans*** are well aware this is not for you; but ***help me hold the fort,*** and let me teach for a brief minute. What I'm saying to you is, *"kill or be killed"* are the words and work of Satan. ***God doesn't operate in this way***. I'm saying it delicately, because you shouldn't live by something God didn't appoint you to live by." ***Your sword should be ready and equipped for the battlefield of God.*** How merciful is His works? Nourish this! David slayed his Giants because God allowed him to do so. There was permission given to slay the giant ***Goliath.*** As it states in scripture, "1st Samuel chapter (17:1-27)" please do read the whole book of 1st Samuel later. ***V:4 A champion went out from the camp of the Philistines, named Goliath, from the Gath, whose height was six cubits and a span.*** He was un-penetrated from the neck down a *"Beast"* amongst men. The giant of a beast shouted out "why have you come out to line up to battle. He then said, *"Choose a man for yourselves and let him come down to see me."* Not only was he not a man but a beast of a giant and told them to choose a man for yourselves, and let him come down to me to do battle. Goliath then marks them and say, *""If he is able to come down here and fight with me and kill me"* then we will be your servants and the same for them. This was nothing but a victory already won in David's ***heart*** as no cowardice lived in him. ***This happens in our everyday life.***

Fight Back -Or- Die for Nothing

The men of Israel were afraid and hidden like cowards. ***David** the son **Ephrathite of Bethlehem** whom had eight children **accepted the challenge** in his heart before he even knew he was going to do **battle.*** David was the youngest of them all and had the heart of a ***warrior,*** but was not in this war with his brothers, but this day when the father sent David to take his brothers and ephah some grain and ten loaves and cheese at the camp, and to see how his brothers were doing to bring back news it wasn't good. David spoke with his brothers and saw that they were hiding from this giant. David was disgusted by his brothers and the men of Israel. The men spoke to David and said, "have you not seen this man who has come up?" He has come to defy Israel; and it shall be that the man who kills him the king will enrich with great riches, will give him his daughter, and give his father's house exemption from taxes in Israel.

Let's do this in laymen's term for those of you whom don't understand the bible yet. This would probably be the younger generation so let me get on your level of communication. In the streets James would run and go get his peoples or would arrive to see his peoples hiding. In which would have angered him and would normally get things popping. ***Did this make since enough!*** David came to check on his brothers to see how they were doing as his father had asked. Just as our parents would ask us, and he found them in a bad way. No one likes to see their siblings bullied nor in a bad way. I know I didn't it was always on and popping in my family. ***Satan loved us doing his bidding.***

Surviving the Enemy

Thank you for changing my ways **Lord!** David said to the men and his brother "what shall be done for the man who kills this philistine and take away the reproach from Israel? Again, they repeated still hiding "so shall it be for the man who kills Goliath, all the riches promised including the king's daughter." Who is this uncircumcised Philistine David nourished in disgust? David sized up all six cubits and span of this giant and said, "you dare defy the armies of the living God!" David shamed by his oldest brother for leaving his sheep in the wilderness to see the battle. Follow your insolence heart David shamed by his brothers *"is there not a cause* that you would die for" David said to his brothers. David's words were reported to Saul. *Saul swore,* "As the Lord lives, and my God lives! David shall not be killed." *David went to battle with permission and put down this giant with a sling shot and a rock.* A Rock *Yep.*

David received all the riches promised including the king's daughter. There's more to this story but this isn't bible study. When God predestines you for something nobody or no one can take that away from you. *Get permission to do battle and your victory may have its purpose.* This is how David killed his enemy, with permission, protection, and the entire armor of God. This book is not telling you to go and kill, because it's a sin and have grave consequences. This here *Heirloom* is to teach you how to do battle with permission and the power of God with the entire armor before you leading your purpose.

Fight Back -Or- Die for Nothing

How Not to Destroy Yourself Fighting the Enemy?

If you're reading my book you haven't lost your mind, and you're not crazy. The enemy wants to drive you psychologically insane. Have you saying things like "I know I'm not crazy" You should be thanking God that you were already of a sound mind before the enemy came into your life. ***One of my favorite scriptures 2 Timothy Chapter 1:7 For God doesn't gives us a spirit of fear but of power and love and of sound mind.*** If anything, I say means anything to you in this here power in your hands, I only ask, "that you go deeper in your relationship with the Lord Jesus Christ." *"Testimony"* We were in training and the attacks were real. "Meditate on the toilet if that's where you pray *"I was taught"* this application. People, Satan is real, and so are the cells under him." So, trust God and believe you can't fight the enemy with your physical self alone. Especially, when the enemy is intentionally trying to destroy you. As human's we respond to stimulus that tempts our flesh. We become destructive or self-destructive, and before you know it-it's too late you've already exchanged hands with the enemy dressed in sheep's clothing. I can't relay this enough; the enemy is sly people. The enemy has cells just sitting around waiting for us to tempt our own flesh. ***We sick, and sick people go to church, that's what they do***. They can't have us if we don't go willingly. *I said, "they can't have us if we don't go willingly.* You heard what God told Satan in the book of Job "*you bet not put your hands on his persons."* Shamefully, some of us go willingly. Got to be the "big shot" and battle it out. Get down and dirty, call the squad pick up those carnal weapons. *I knew I'll get your attention right here.* Now if you're asking what a carnal weapon is *(I)* want you to stop reading right now and go look up carnal weapon for you will never mistake the meaning again. This here power in your hands will wait for you to return with nourishment. These words aren't going anywhere and I'm assuming this is your personal copy.

Surviving the Enemy

This book is too good to be borrowing, you're not going to want to return it to its rightful owner. **This Heirloom in your hands is like being in the HOV lane with God.** Do not borrow it, get your own copy for your family's sake. You can't go up against the enemy without God and let me tell you why? Because it's God vs. Everything. God vs. Gantsa's, murders, dealers, rapist, molesters, addiction, lairs, thieves, illnesses, bullies, and all else the enemy can come up with. **Don't make a move without King Jesus.**

That's why we're in spiritual warfare people. I hope you're still with me, because I'm going to tell you how gangster our God is "He gave his only son" as a sacrifice for our sins. I don't know a man of this statute, and selflessness that would die for me but Jesus! **Now that's Gangster!** *Selah* that! For our existence God gave his only son. **Oh my**, I hope you didn't miss the colossal point being made here. Most humans I'm sorry to state, "would awaken with their first breath and would not give thanks to God." We're moving through the atmosphere like he didn't make it happen. He "Literally" created the earth in six days and rested on the sabbath. **That's Gantsa!** As humans we self-destruct when our backs are against the wall, give up, quit before the battle even starts. We'll let me tell you this "the same way you got your hook up" *my God got my back*. When Satan came for me, I meditated after the fact. I bet, I wished, I thought about meditating before the attack. **Hmmm.** Meditating before an attack is Gods way of preparing you for a victory man can't give you. **My God stick with me.** See, **if you allow God to prepare you before your attack**, and believe me, one is coming, and depending on how personal the attack is when the enemy arrives you will be victorious. The enemy won't even get close enough to deter your weapon of "FAITH" if you just meditate and do things Gods way. **You see,** when you have faith, it's unwavering and unmoved. Meaning if some ill-intentioned person walks up to you pointing a gun at you, you're liable all-powerful to take that man's power.

Fight Back -Or- Die for Nothing

A power given as a gift, and one uses it for harm, ***"Oh My"*** that same power that be in you, the Holy Spirit will be strip from your enemy, as you belong to the Lord Jesus Christ, and not the enemy. When the Holy Spirit gives permission and power (WOE) to those that come up against you and yours. No matter how hard they try, if God doesn't want you harmed it isn't going to happen. ***God will tire your enemy out to a position where the enemy will have realized if I can't beat you, I would like to join you!*** God said he would make your enemies your friends and appoint you charged. Lord Jesus speak to your children through this power.

Selah!

CHAPTER THREE
How to Protect Your Family from The Enemy During Spiritual Warfare

This is where it gets real people! All bets are off the table, anything, and I mean anything is fair game to the enemy. The enemy cares nothing about your family. Meaning your entire family is at risk. You must know that you have something that Satan wants! The power of prayer is the strongest weapon to use against the enemy. Pray your family in the hands of Jesus Christ. The Holy Spirit will consume you and the very body you pray from for protection. Prayer is a cure to the cells of the enemy. The enemy doesn't want to be cured. The enemy wants to cause illnesses to everything and everyone that allows its transfer. It's like an antibiotic fighting a foreign entity. For some of us, we know the devil very well, because we have had victory in Christ. To those of you that don't even know the sacrifices made for you and your sins, you better take cover quick. The devil will try anything it wants, ***against*** the covenant of Christ Jesus. You have got to know what Faith feels and looks like to survive what's coming.

Ask me what faith looks like? God told me to tell you, it looks like a sacrifice. A great sacrifice just like ***Jesus***. The greatest sacrifice of them all! Faith looks like you and me standing in humility in the blood of Jesus Christ confessing our relationship with our Lord our Savior the ***Christ***. Faith feels like humanity coming together for the greater good. ***My God, people I can't just stop here,*** "Faith is just one power that stands against many in persecution." Faith is you and me in this world, waiting for each of us to take our divine appointed positions to do what we were born to do. ***I said' and I quote myself,*** "what we were born to do" not what "Saturday night" calls you to do. In your ability and power, the Lord trusted in you to bring in this world future kings, and queens as they too are destined to multiply after you. ***You have responsibilities that need your divine attention.***

Fight Back -Or- Die for Nothing

I'm about to leave you with great nourishment, and you must not doubt its clarity. ***Your children are a split image of you, as you were of your parents.*** If you feel there's something different about you, or felt there's always been something different about you growing up from everybody else, and still is, that's because you belong to ***King Jesus.*** God has different plans for you. "You can't take everybody where God is taking you. Are you ready, ***here it is:*** "you are doubting the gift of the Holy Spirit that resides in you." ***You have got to get this!*** You have a *power* in you God has allowed you to pass down from generation to generation to protect your family from the likes and cells of the enemy.

People, it's deeper than the surface of it all. Satan didn't just decide to pick on you. We have been the target of the enemy for centuries. To find out prayer and the Will of God were the only things I needed to fight, and steadfast against the enemy, fear and the unexpected, I only wish I identified my gifts sooner. Say it with, ***"God is always on time"*** the enemy wasn't ready for this here power. My God, ***OMG*** again, it's the best feeling you'll ever gather in this life attaining a victory that belongs to God. I'm exposing this power now, as I don't want you to wait until you're 20, 30, 40, and 50 to discover you have the power of God in you to defeat any weapon that comes up against your persons, bloodline, and your purpose. ***Let's tap into that power right now!***

Surviving the Enemy

When you receive victory through Christ Jesus and you didn't have to lift a finger against the enemy, you better know His name when He pulls you through. ***You better believe it wasn't Craig, and Black from the block you chill with all the time.*** It was God, King of all kings that got Gangster for you and yours. God vs. Gangsters ***"what does the opposition really want"*** God has victory over everything. Again ***"what does the opposition really want!"*** This is the stance you take when you know you have a personal relationship with your Lord and Savior. I hope He doesn't get me for calling Him Gangster "He is after all the original (OG)." I can go deeper here, but I'm going to move on.

It's Best

Amen….

Fight Back -Or- Die for Nothing

How to Protect Your Psychological Thinking from the Enemy

First, I would like to thank my Lord and Savior, *again* Jesus Christ for speaking to me in a clear voice. If it wasn't for Him loving me so much and informing me of His unconditional love through clear voice you wouldn't be reading this sacred piece of work destined to be here even after He calls me home. *2 Timothy 1:7 (again) for God does not give us a spirit of fear but of love and power and of sound mind.* People when you have sound mind, can't nobody make you "crazy" in the Lord. *Nobody!* Direct yourself to scripture if anybody ever tries to make you crazy. It pleased my soul to know I wasn't crazy after all, just Gifted. *Lol.* Mathew chapter 5:8 Blessed are the pure in heart, for they shall see God. It's a joy to share one of my experiences with my Savior with you. *I will make it quick hopefully.* It's so good, "like Jesus seasoning" *Nourish this!*

My Deep breath, in 2013 I was thrown in jail, persecuted, and charged with outlandish charges of *"Murder I, & II"* I told the Lord in jail, the devil was lying on me. With nothing to lose I opened my heart to God in my cell and spoke as if He was right there. I prayed and asked God from the very pit they placed me to consider my heart and see the truth. I didn't yet have a solid relationship with my God, but I prayed for mercy, as there was no other aide in my life. *People,* I was at a high point in my life. *Too high,* for the likes of the enemy, and was hit hard, pinned from all four sides with no way out. At least, that's what the enemy wanted me to think. I was in graduate school newly married, beautiful daughter, promoted to supervisor at my job making good money, and envy of all that hated me. My life was turned upside down in one night, thrown into jail to never be heard from again.

Surviving the Enemy

People, I spoke to God often and said to Him, "you did not open all these doors in my life for it to end like this" I said to Him, "Father I am not guilty of the things they say, but I am guilty of being a drunkard. If I'm to be punish for anything let it be, for that, for which my behavior was unacceptable. I'm now eight years clean in my sobriety. ***Stay with me*** I'm taking you down a very bumpy road I wish you not to travel.

Somewhere along the lines of being a drunkard, I say, ***"somewhere"*** because being a drunkard you get use to the excuses, such as: ***"I don't remember"*** after you have caused all hell the night before. You know what I'm talking about! At least that's how they're going to ***TELL*** your story. You don't see it, until your drunkard-ness puts you in a situation where you're unable to psychologically think for yourself. Yet, we make it easy for someone else to tell our story, testifying against you with their version of *your* story, your life and then call you a liar to your face, because you were too drunk to remember. ***You bet your last dollar I stop drinking and got sober quick! The devil will not tell my story nor lie on me ever again.***

Thankyou

God!

JB!

*PLEASE I BEG OF YOU
STOP
KILLING EACH OTHER
YOU'RE FIGHTING
WITHOUT THE ARMOR
OF GOD!*

Surviving the Enemy

I was fighting for my life, I fasted my apples, your apples, and my cell mate's apples. I got so close to my Lord & Savior in the fight for my life, that my incarceration turned around in my favor. ***The enemy came into my life and sent the cells of Satan into my home with a full fledge attack of ill intentions I wasn't aware.*** There was a **Battle** in my home! **People**, I saw the devil and an Angel in my home fighting for my life. ***What makes me so special that God would send someone to my aide.*** What I witnessed what you only see in movies. But there, right in my home was a battle for my life. Fighting back wasn't the answer, it was the way I fought back after thrown in jail that turned in my favor. What I saw that night followed me the rest of my days to ensure me it wasn't just the alcohol that night. The fight of my life was real and God was chastening me to acknowledge there is Heaven on Earth, and no amount of consumption could ever make me delusional to hide the presence and power of the Lord in my life.

People, this beautiful golden spirit came to me in my cell just when I was about give up, and had a hold of my soul pushing it back down within me as I laid on the bottom bunk and said to me, "not yet." The **second** time a visitor came *"stay with me people"* I was in the shower weeping hoping to sink through the cracks of the drain, but there was no way out. **Somehow,** while in the shower I ended up in my living room where the battle went down. **Come On**, I'm walking you through my experience with the Lord Himself that is now in this book as a living *"testimonies."* I looked up from crying within the shower in jail, and there I was suddenly no longer in jail, but stirring out of my living room window. There was a white dove hovering flapping its wings stirring at me, and right there formed the shape of what looked like a human being. **People,** I opened my front door and my **Savior Jesus Christ** walked in, and I collapsed in his arms never hitting my living room floor. **Oh,** people I didn't want to let Him go. To feel His arms around me made nothing else in this world matter. Not my child, mother, husband, family, friends nothing mattered.

Fight Back -Or- Die for Nothing

People He didn't say anything He just held me. Even right now I weep. I Hope you're still reading, "I came to in the shower" whimpering like a baby needing formula. I accepted I was losing my mind. Prior to this experience I went to court five different times, and each time a different prosecutor tried to persecute me, and every time I cried and muttered *not guilty*. That Thursday when I returned from court, I called home to break a promise I made to my daughter that I wasn't coming home. She asked, *"why mommy"* and I said pleading guilty to man wasn't in God's plan for me. I told her we're going to wait this one out." When I came out of the shower, I wanted something so badly to help me sleep, but the infirmary was closed for the weekend. *Let's stop for a minute here.* I don't want you to misunderstand nothing I'm sharing as these are facts with dates and times.

   Recap, I really thought I was going crazy. After court that Thursday I pleaded not guilty came back to the jail and prepared myself to sit for six months on a *1325* hold. If you've been where I been, then you know what a *1325* hold means. *But God, has the last say over any judgement that cometh against His children.* I just shared with you my transition from the jail shower to my living room. *Stay with me people!* My God, *Friday* I woke up and felt *unbothered*, "it disturbed me I was different" I felt lighter in my storm. I called home like normally, but even spoke differently. *Saturday*, I rested for the first time in a long time. I really got some sleep this day undisturbed. I called home later that day, and my daughter said, "mommy I been waiting on you to call all day." *Talking about the voice of an angel in your time of need.* Sunday, I went to worship and received the word. I didn't care who was giving it, I just yearned to hear God's promise. *Let's stop for a minute.* I've come to notice that everyone has their favorite pastor, minister, or guest speaker they want to receive the word from. I get it, I really do, but people when you have a divine relationship with the Lord, *it doesn't matter who the messenger is that delivers.*

Surviving the Enemy

You're going to steadfast to receive the word from any appointed messenger of Lord when you have a relationship with Christ Jesus. The barriers will be no more when you get that relationship with the Lord. It doesn't matter your religion all bodies of religion make up the body of Christ Jesus. I fight with my own family to get to the sanctuary. My family be mad at me Sunday mornings fighting with them to get to church.

Let's get back to it I can drift sometimes. Leaving service that Sunday was the first Sunday service I attended and knew that my life would never be the same. Monday came and I didn't need nothing to help me sleep, because God had lifted the weight that held me down since my entrance to **DC Jail.** I woke up feeling twenty pounds lighter. This is where your enemy will know your Saviors name! Tuesday morning around ***4am*** early the guard came calling names for court appearances. They called my name, but I just laid there knowing it was a mistake, as I just left court Thursday, pleaded not guilty and prepared myself to sit for the next six months under the ***1325 hold.*** The inmate across the hall from me came in and said ***"Walker"*** they called your name for court I told her it was a mistake, "I went already last week." She insisted I see the guard to make sure. I went to the guard and said I already been to court I don't go back for six months, and the guard said, you ***Walker?*** Yes, I replied. The guard stated in a very nasty way "I really don't care if you go, or not your name is on this list for a court appearance scheduled this morning." I went back downstairs and laid down. ***"Who she talking to"*** I said with not a care, and again came the cell mate from across the hall saying to me, "come on you got to go." Have you ever heard; God don't make no mistakes" ***He didn't!*** I went and whelped the entire ride to the courthouse. I don't have to tell you I gained a name for myself while incarcerated. ***Cry-baby,*** I could hear other inmates say, ***"that's all she does is cry."*** I just wished they knew what I knew. They were comfortable and content with chains and bars and scars.

Fight Back -Or- Die for Nothing

I wanted my scars to mean something, I wanted those chains broken, I wanted those bars open, and people King Jesus came for me. No bars, or chains will hold you no longer. I went to court and when I got there, I didn't see my attorney. It was a stand in attorney and a stand in Prosecutor. I was snotty nose tears flowing saying *NOT* guilty walking in, and my statement wasn't going to change. People, the attorney received me in an angelic way. It was unreal and the prosecutor steadfast with remanding me in jail with no humility. *The attorney said stop crying you're going home. People,* I cried even harder. The judge handed me tissue from behind the bench and said I'm releasing you into the *HISP* program. People to this day *HISP* stands for *"Highly Intelligent Supernatural Person".* I never went back to the that jail. I was taken to the release center of what used to be *DC General Hospital.*

    Outside it was wet, snowing and cold I wanted to walk home, but I just got *Confirmation* that my God is who He say He is, and He told me to call my husband to get here and get me. I did, he did and people when I got home, you're not going to believe this, it was in the same spot I stood when I opened my door and Christ Jesus came in and caught me in His arms never letting me hit the floor. *You see,* I wasn't going crazy, or losing myself psychologically self-hearing things, seeing things, and teleporting my weight. *My Father the Lord Jesus Christ, the Holy Spirit, God and the Word all in one came into a facility meant to house prisoners, adhered to my prayers knowing the truth already, looked in my heart and said, "I have dominion over your life and what I say will be the last written in stone"* **Selah.** *People,* I hit the floor in my house yelling Jesus and whelped for hours and then *Days*. I wasn't going crazy after all I was experiencing the power of the true living God. I'm ending this chapter with this "don't *EVER* doubt the gifts and power that are within you that connects you to the one and only living God."

Surviving the Enemy
𝒯𝒽𝑒 𝒮𝓅𝒾𝓇𝒾𝓉𝓊𝒶𝓁 𝒯𝒾𝓂𝑒 𝒪𝓊𝓉 - 5/07/2018

People, "It's Hard Being a Christian" I love that God "loves me unconditionally" where would I be if I didn't know this. Where would we be if we didn't know His Love & Grace for our lives. "I don't want to know" it's hard being a Christian, but I live for the challenge. I have no choice. ***Fight for something or die for nothing!*** Who are we, as a people, to let God's sacrifice of His only son go in vain? This is not just a story to tell our children, "it's the hard truth of our Father's sacrifice for our sins."

   People, the deeper I get into writing this book the more challenges that come up against me, but no matter what, I won't stop until these chapters are completed, shared, and the sacrifices my King has made for my life are felt with no mistakes about His presence. **When God is for you, then whom can be against you.**

   A copy of this very power you hold in your hands was at one point held by a professor, ***"that didn't want the bondage, that didn't want the bondage, I say that didn't want the bondage and strongholds it held on me released."*** Refused to return it unless I moved as the enemy wanted me to move, and do as the enemy wanted me to do. Thank God for back-ups ***"God did not renew a fool to stay a fool"*** Amen. Professor P. You hold on to that copy, as only I and God can finish me and my work. ***Selah.*** You can hold my ***degree***, over ***charge*** my tuition, ***threaten me***, and ***my family***, but you can't stop this ***truth***. I won't ***expose*** you in this book!

Thank you, Jesus,
***"Fear is a Gift"* Conquer It!**

JB.

Fight Back -Or- Die for Nothing
How to Protect Your Job and Home from The Enemy
(Pray & Selah)

I know I don't have to tell you this, especially if you're seasoned in Christ. ***Hmmmmm*** I'm so hungry right now - it sounds delicious *"God" can only taste better being praised out of your mouth.* Renewed in His Grace reasoned and rebased. If this was a Christian season it would sell out every shelf filled, because that's just how good God is in my life. ***People,*** you protect your stability and home with an unwavering steadfast. When it comes to your home *'Nehemiah 4:13-14" I station the people by their clans, with their swords, their spears, and their bows.* And I looked and arose and said to the nobles and to the officials and to the rest of the people, "Do not be afraid of them. **Remember the Lord,** who is great and awesome, and fight for your brothers, your sons, your daughters, your wives, and your **homes**. Let me translate this for those that need **season** for the **reason**. Let no man enter your castle unwelcome to cast dismay upon units of your family. When anointed in Christ you are a part of Christ, His brethren, His Covenant, His Grace, His Mercy. Know that you are the sons and daughters of the True living God. ***People,*** if you know this, and walk like you know this, and live like you know this, your enemy will know this! They're going to learn whom your Father, true King Lord and Savior is in your mind, body, and soul. ***Amen***

People' pray like you never prayed before and praise God for Jesus. Praise like every praise is brand new. Don't run from this "I promise you'll be able to teach from just this piece alone." God doesn't ask where our tithing and offerings come from, and He doesn't tell us to do bad things to get it, but we do it! I'm not going to be a hypocrite here, I said *"we."* We should be grateful every sin isn't punished. We should be praising God for keeping us and not casting us where we know we belong. We should be praising Him for pulling us out of those messy situations, strongholds that should've ended us.

Surviving the Enemy

The physicality of this world got our flesh so covered from the truth, we don't even say thank you when God answers our hearts desires and request. I'll say it for you. **Thank-you Jesus!!!**

    People, we already have the promise of this physical world. We have got to get past the physicality of this world that leads our flesh to turn a blind eye to the promise of the true living God. Money is enjoyed here on earth. You can't take it with you. Not the clothes, shoes, cars, houses, money, but hold on, you can't take your man's and them either. As much as we might not want to die, or dine alone, everybody leaves this earthly plain the way they came in "alone." Even (twins) go their own ways in life. When our Lord and Savior has a plan for our lives, we can't take everyone with us to where God is leading us. I don't know about you, but I prefer to see family and friends during the holidays and special occasions. If God says, "you can't have what He has for me" don't try to plot my demise to get rid of me. ***God saideth your plot will turn in my favor.***

    Just as He Promises Me Life,

    Amen/Selah.

CHAPTER FOUR
What Do You Need to Survive the Enemy?
A Mustered Seed of Faith!

Isn't it something when the enemy comes knocking and fear becomes you? *Oh' what a feeling and I'm not speaking of "Tony the Tiger" Great!* Fear is one of the most astonishing feelings in the world. Let's think about this for a minute, when was the last time you were fearful of something, or someone and your fear became you. *Yes,* keeping it real with the response of fear. Fear makes you have all types of symptoms such as bubble guts, trembling, sweating, stuttering trying to get your words together, and my favorite symptom of them all is to completely shut down. *Fear does amazing things people.*

You have to remember, if you know having a relationship with the Lord's word, scripture, then you should also know, again, *"2nd Timothy Chapter 1. V7 "For God does not gives us a spirit of fear but of power and love and sound mind."* I experienced this fear at great levels and before I was taught this very scripture' fear always knew how to hit me. So, when I was taught *2nd Timothy*, I was astonished and felt like an epiphany had surge through my flesh. *Stay with me*, it was the *experience people, that connected my conscious to my subconscious, and my subconscious knocked on the door of revelations, and Jesus invited me in. I hope you didn't miss the colossal point here.* That feeling you get when you assume something is what it is, and then here comes that spiritual ally confirming your greatest fear, truth, and assumption. Isn't it something how, what we do as human beings after receiving confirmation, "we fall back and do nothing" that's not what *"Surviving the Enemy"* is all about! This is where you take fear and experience it, steadfast in it, walk in it, nourish it, and stare fear right in its ugly face. Fear makes me mad sometimes, but fear is greatly needed. Why? *Because everything you want is on the other side of fear.*

Surviving the Enemy

People you got to monopolize fear, strategized fear, and become fearful to overcome it. Fear comes in various forms and most of the time it comes from within us, giving life to its very foundation. The only thing you need to know about fear, "is not to RUN from it" because, by the time fear catches up with you, you'll be too tired to fight back. ***Stay with me I'm taking you somewhere with this here truth!*** To fear man is a disappointment to God, as he is the only man, was human, and now the Holy Spirit that you should be fearful. God has made man in his image and has made certain we as humans know the difference between man and the true living God. That should hit home for some folks. On a more personal note, we're too busy entertaining what we can get from man but won't entertain the promise of the true living God. If you're attracted to man then you should know the attraction to the true living King, as man is made in His image. ***He made to woman too!*** Wo-Man. ***Ok***, I won't start any trouble, nor raise the Glass Ceiling here.

Don't want to escape the real intention of this truth.

JB...

Fight Back -Or- Die for Nothing

There would never be no confusion on who to follow if you a had relationship with the Lord Jesus Christ. There would never be no confusion on who to adhere if you have a relationship with Jesus Christ. There would be no mistake in who to be fearful if you had a relationship with the true living God. When God intervenes, you will know it wasn't man that brought you out of the pit, the Lion's Den, the Fire, and help you defeat your Giant whom is lite weight for God, and no problem for you to conquer when you have a Divine relationship with God. People I got to share yet another *testimony* in this chapter.

People I was in that pit accused of murdering my husband, my husband's son, and my husband friend. Because of these terrible accusations I was thrown in jail to rot until I caved to the accusations.

Let me tell you something about being born, and then reborn again "when you're born your life has already been predestined to happen the way it's turning out. *The good, the bad, and the ugly.* We have experience living in our past lives and occasionally have that "déjà vu" experience that reminds us of a repeated experience, but for the mimesis of it, we can't recall it. That's because it's an opportunity to respond differently than you did in your past life. *My God* don't miss this, old folk's call it *"spiritual warfare"* something that has happened before you arrived here on earth. Clinicians today call it the *"here and now"* affect. People, fear is a gift and to master it you have to start paying attention to the way your body responds to situations, persons, environments, and for the life you have right now, please stop and ask God to give you guidance before listening to other humans. *"People, how many of us have them, friends, ones we can depend on."* How many of us have them? Let Me Stop! Again, "God said trust Him" not humans. Nowhere in the bible does God say, "Trust Human's" God said "to lean on Him for all understanding and not yourself.

Surviving the Enemy

People, that's what I did in the pit I was thrown. I leaned on God and told Him to look into my heart for facts, and that's exactly what the King of Kings did. He already knew the truth. He knew I could've handled things differently if I wasn't a drunkard. He also knew I didn't do what I was accused.

    I was released when all odds were against me, and not only was I released, but my enemies were no longer an active problem, but they still preyed upon my persons, and knew better than to touch His anointed. I can't stress this enough, when you have a relationship with God, or has had a significant experience with God such as myself. Nothing in this world can change that *"Nothing!"* I'm not saying this to brag, but when God Himself comes for you and frees you from a bondage, cage, or chains you are forever linked. When you're linked people will recognize it and will either accept it and welcome the change in you, or they will make it their life's work to see you back in that pit God rescued you from. *Just as God is alive Satan is too!*

    Walk like you want to know God. Invite Him in your Life, give your everything to Him as an offering and I promise you as He promised me eternal life "you will not walk in fear, you will nourish it, you will know how to respond to fear" and then you will conquer the steadfast of fear.

Trust God with Everything!

JB.

Fight Back -Or- Die for Nothing
When Will the Enemy Attack?

Whenever you're not looking! For revelations will expose in thy time when a coward is condemned to hellfire along with murderers and anything else that causes hell on earth. Its evil will try to take everything in his/her walkabout to hell. I'm going to be brief, as it simply means don't be so modest to your adversaries.' Especially one whom lacks courage and succumb to fear and will do anything to free him/herself from the likes of evil, even sacrificing a friend. ***It's ok though!*** After reading this powerful tool, courage will become you. I'm speaking here of the coward that plots on the weak, and prey on the unaware. I'm speaking here of the human that awakens as a king and lie down as a coward by night, and who's life has been shortened because of the cowardly act committed from the time he/she awakened in the morning, and by the time they laid their nasty @sses down to sleep still with God's breath in their body.

*People' **stay with me***, I'm going somewhere with this power, the same power that's within you. Even with our nastiness He still allows us life. That's just how awesome our King **REALLY** is. There's nothing short, nor lacking of the one true God. Whom works relentlessly for our nasty @ss sins. The cussing spirit persuaded me to put emphasis on the statement! ***Selah that!*** How do we fix this, how can we as a (people) change for our God whom gave His only son for our nasty sins? Not by yourself, I didn't do it by myself, and I know you can't do by yourself, and God doesn't want you taking on the enemy alone by yourself. God wants you to put on the entire armor of Him, and then nourish your response to the enemy. Sure enough, the enemy is going to respond, and if not now, you can bet your lifespan the enemy will respond later.

Surviving the Enemy

People' when you put on the whole armor of God the enemy will eventually be defeated and realize something supernatural is happening outside of their power. The enemy won't know it's the supernatural happening, because the enemy is too blinded by cockiness, stupidity, and blind determination set to destroy what it can't have. God said, *"let the enemy attack"* your response will seem harmless with the most powerful impact. *Nourish that for a minute people.* Taste that! *Again,* when you belong to God "all your problems are lite in Christ Jesus" let me say this again *"when you belong to God" All Your Problems Are Lite in Christ Jesus.* I mentioned this in earlier chapters, just when the enemy can't get to you anymore, the enemy will sure enough go after your children, elderly parents, friends, pets, home, cars, opportunities, finances, and anything that makes you happy. Everything I just mentioned you better pray over. *You better pray over it!*

People, I can't stress it enough *"self-exposing"* again, when God brought me out of the pit, it pissed off a lot of people, and sure enough they went after my child in her school. She was sexually assaulted by two occupants with security cameras, and security on every floor and exit. This isn't a (HOW) anymore, but a *(WHY)*. When I tell you, they didn't get the response they wanted from me to violate me, and throw me back in prison, it confused every piece of knowledge they plotted and ever bestowed against me. *My God I'm leading you to an understanding past your means of vengeance!* The enemies plot on my life was a part of God's plan to prosper me and my family.

Fight Back -Or- Die for Nothing

I know exactly what you're saying, "let that had been my child, I'll be going right back to jail." *These idiots weren't aware what God had done to me, for me, that CHANGED me in jail.* Don't touch His anointed! He said "Don't do it." And they couldn't help themselves and touched my child." They learned quickly she was under the same covering as I. *WOE to those that come up against His covering!*

People, a second *testimony* of God speaking to me in clear voice mentioned in an earlier chapter. God told me to maintain in clear voice, and at this time I was fighting my daughter's case and my case at the same time with a *box* on my ankle. On the following Sunday me and my family attended church services at our home church, and this singer *Jonathan McReynolds was performing "Help me Maintain"* and I couldn't believe my ears as it was symbolic to me that *"Help me Maintain"* was enough confirmation that God had my back. Lyrics in the song stuck out like a saw dumb, as God had very recently spoke to me, prior to this revelation and told me to, "maintain and read Him" as to what I was going through, the Lyrics *"As soon as I walk out that door someone may be on a different page"* helped me nourish the confirmation I needed to really maintain the storm that came up against me and mine.

People, when God sends you somewhere unbeknownst to your conscious, and it was liberating that you went, and you retained something, it's simply God communicating with you to open up your unconscious mind to what you can't see, but can feel His unconditional love for your life on this earth. I'm still surviving the enemy, and I'm here to tell you to *"maintain"* in everything you do when responding to the enemy. Remember Satan has tricks that can turn *you* into the enemy and have you sitting in jail wondering how did I get here, and why for the life of me I couldn't maintain against ploy that challenge my existence.

Surviving the Enemy

People, you need to know the only reason the enemy is after you, is because you're more powerful then you acknowledge the God in you, and the fact that the enemy want's something from you means there is power within you. ***Come on stay with me.*** If the enemy wants something from you, ask God what does this bamma want from you? God will reveal very clearly who's causing the problem, and what to do about the problem. ***When you're powerful and don't know your God given gifts, the enemy wants to keep it that way.*** Armor up and pray a hedge of protection over everything in your life with God leading, and I promise you, it will be the most difficult task the enemy can encounter coming up against you and yours.

That Is A Promise!

JB...

Fight Back -Or- Die for Nothing

Who Will the Enemy Attack?

I feel like I should remove this chapter, but I won't because I can't over emphasize how petty the cells of the enemy are when they attack. From scripture perspectives, Psalm 5 "What to do when under attack" take refuge in the Lord as your righteous defender. Let your eyes deceive you not! Do not respond to your enemy's plot, but master it, and be not fool by the enemy, but be a fool for God as He love's fool's and children. *I know your thoughts are stacking up. For every response to this scripture you could've paid your tithings and offerings for the entire year and get a tax right off for contributions.* Let me be the first to save your life, or at least save you from some jail time! *Psalm 5:1-2* you are being a David I will strongly advise you to give repeated appeals to the Lord God to consider your groaning. Heed the sound of your cry for help, and make sure to wept from your gut. Don't pretend to have it all together, because that utters you don't need the King of Kings whom has made you in His image.

For the young men out there in the world cutting your brethren's life short, you are no way a tool for these streets, and the destruction of yourself. *There's only a 2% chance of surviving being gangster.* Don't be that 98% and don't be the 2% that lives to teach from jail how bad decisions took moored than 50% of their lives away. God is, the only one above the mountain top whom given His only son for our sins, and is the only (OG) I know. God sacrificed His only son! He didn't murder him for us to live. He sacrificed His only son for you to overcome your flesh that leads to sin. God doesn't need you despicably trying to repeat His sacrifice by killing his sons and daughters made in His image.

Surviving the Enemy

Again, you are no gangster, you were a King before you decided to take life over your selfish identity so undeveloped. Now even farther from your true appointment in this life. ***People,*** taking refuge from those streets will earn you the time you should've used to master your enemy. As valid as a threat may appear, ducking "lil Curtis" is not hiding, it's called taking refuge until the enemy isn't bearing arms/carnal weapons, that you know, he's telling everybody he's looking for you to cause you serious harm, or possibly death. Young people use refuge to nourish your situation and then decide how you want to respond to the enemy.

So, what does this mean, you're thinking? ***Again,*** use your time wisely responding to the enemy. I will leave you with this "my enemies, enemy are my friends." This power in your hand's is not based on the matrix's or Neil choosing a red pill or the blue pill. It comes a time in your life where you must decide what side of the fence you want to be on. I'll take the good over the bad any day. Side note: ducking (Lil) Curtis until he's not bearing arms is time enough to nourish your response, an Armored Godly response should be your only option. If naysayer utter anything else, they're hiding behind your purpose even waiting to walk it for you. ***Nourish all decision that will change your life.***

Fight Back -Or- Die for Nothing

Where Will the Enemy Attack?

Right on your home front! Keep your eyes peeled as the enemy will come to your front door in disguise asking for you, your children, spouse, mother, father, grandparents and even your pet. The enemy will come to your job, church, family function, children's school, your school, doctor's appointments, restaurants, movies, concerts, walking, jogging, fishing, boating, camping, swimming, beach, games, events, anywhere you are the enemy can and will appear. ***Satan doesn't discriminate people, but we do this very well to each other.*** The enemy uses us to do its bidding because the enemy is too coward to show its ugly face, and when the enemy does decide to show up, "remember" as I mentioned earlier, the enemy only comes after you when you're close to your breakthrough, being victorious, celebrating or simply enjoying life. You must know that your ancestors gave the enemy hell, as hell is hot and still is in spiritual warfare. Their assurance is to make sure you continue to fight with the entire armor of God when the enemy comes against you and yours. Be always prepared in prayer with the entire armor of God, and I promise you the enemy again, won't stand a chance against you. ***People,*** the same impact this powerful tool teaches you, please teach this to your children or anybody old enough to be taught. It can save their lives, as God promises eternal life. ***Amen.***

CHAPTER FIVE

Steadfast with The Enemy - Forgive the Cussing Spirit

This is not to say forget everything above this chapter. This here, is to say, **"Stuff Happens"** when stepping out of your front door. Again, in the words and lyrics of Jonathan McReynolds "God Help Me Maintain" and steadfast for this chapter. By real life examples: if you step out your door and Lil Curtis is there with a carnal weapon pointed at your person, shock will not become you, but the **power of God will come out of you,** not only to save your life, but to spear that man his life as well. **That's right!** Spear that man his life if you can! You nor Curtis is not the living God! No one has a right to take life nor decide another human must die today. Only God has had the permanency of making this decision, and because of His Sacrifice of His **only son** Jesus, our nasty @sses have a place to breath to Rome on this earth He so created for life to multiply. Steadfast with Lil Cutis, or whomever the enemy pops up to be. Let them know if it wasn't for your relationship with God the tables would have changed the outcome. Then call the police and have their nasty @ss arrested and press full charges against them as they woke this morning trying to take your life through strife. **But God!** People you can slay your Giants and pray at the same time.

You can be a David, Moses, Paul, and A Daniel. When you have
Favor in the Lord your enemies have **Godly problems** they could've never suspected. This read is for you, your children, and the young at heart. Why do I say the young at heart, because we were all immature one time or another in our lives, and those coming behind us awaits teachings. **Volunteers anyone, anyone!** This here power in your hands will help you teach a powerful truth. *As a matter of fact, gift wrap it now, and wait for it. You will give it at the right time. Amen!*

Fight Back -Or- Die for Nothing

People, we are so challenged by the enemy, our flesh leads us right to the enemy. *Trust I know*, I have been foul, nasty, messy, and conflictual with thy own self. *But God!* God found me worthy to be saved. I didn't get it the first time, second, third, fourth, fifth or the sixth time around. He kept coming after me and saving me from me. *Fighting the enemy is one thing, but when you're your own worst enemy OMG is the only cure.* God is a God of second chances, a God of mercy, is a God of power, and a God of Favor just for you. If you're thinking gets to failing you along the lines of thinking *"I always get away with it"* or *"I never get caught"* you're more delusional than the foundation you're pulling the roots of your stinking thinking. When I say steadfast that means steadfast against your delusional thinking, and the lies you tell yourself, and especially what you put in the atmosphere. *What you put out there comes back around.* I don't know about you, but I want God around when my enemy thinks about me. *Amen*

It's like a new track, it's either going to sell or not sell. The difference here is when you're selling something, make sure it's going to change a people. *Make sure it's going to impact the lives of those needing a Godly interruption in their lives.* God didn't renew you to sell biscuits, He renewed you, and me to renew a world that's drowning in murder, rape, addiction, incest, adultery, lies, treachery, and every sin not mentioned. He calls for us to steadfast and be a people that can change a nation, city, home, church, these streets, communities, families, and the way we approach the enemy. Steadfast in everything not God sent. *Be a stead-fasting people and help me change the way we steadfast in everything not God sent.*

Surviving the Enemy

Leave Your Mark on The Enemy
This Is So Imperative!

This isn't about winning or losing. This is about letting the enemy know who it is dealing with! I've been victimized, I have revictimized, I have been arrested, re-arrested, I have a criminal record, I was an alcoholic since the age of 12 years old, I now have eight years of sobriety. I have been knocked down, I have gotten back up, I have been cheated on, I too have cheated, I have been molested as a child, and now have power over those people that have molested me, I have been betrayed, and betrayed in return. *Again*, this is not about winning and losing this is about letting the enemy know, been there and done that, and well-nourished in the attacks of the enemy. When I say (I) "I mean I" I have been broken and put back together. *I have been beaten only to be healed.* I have been thrown in the pit for the one and only true living God to come and rescue me. I have been cast aside, and found by the one and only true living God to say, *"not yet."*

You see, it doesn't matter what another human being has to say about you. It matters what the one and true living God has rescued you from to tell your story. This is imperative *stay with me*. What matters now is, "who am I" who are you after Surviving the Enemy. I am the child of God who was **pushed into a train** in Union station and an Angel by the name of St. Paul told me to hold on. My first encounter ever with a spiritual being not in our realm. I'm the girl that blew up in my mother's kitchen and walked out of the flam with a mark to remind me of what God pulled me through. **Doctor's at Children's Hospital** where I stayed for three months in the burn unit said, *"my entire body should've burned"* but didn't.

Fight Back -Or- Die for Nothing

I'm the child of God whose mother traded her for a six pack of beer and made it back alive and still moved mountains of love for her. ***But God!*** I'm the child of God who was child barren and my family made fun and marked me for it. ***I'm the child of God whom He giveth a child knowing my heart yearned for motherhood.*** She reminds me every day of the gift that keeps on giving. ***Especially*** on ***Mother's Day.*** I'm the child of God whom you shot at, but I steadfast. My cousin came and got me. ***A David in my Life.*** I'm the child of God you raped and beaten. I'm the child of God whom you lied on. I'm the child of God whose parents suffered greatly at the expense of you trying to get to me. ***I'm the child of God you set up.*** I'm the child of God you tried to have incest with. I'm the child of God that knows what you have done. ***I'm the child of God you tried to come up against and admitted knowing my strength.*** I am His anointed, His daughter, and He is my King, and I am still here, because He saideth and permitted my appointments in this life. My King, my God, my Father, the one and only true living God that lives in me and you, gets the last say over our works and walkabout in this life.

Surviving the Enemy

People, I'm here to tell you **FACTS,** the same power that lives in me is in you. **The enemy wants to keep you silent.** Let the enemy know who you are, let the enemy know who you belong. Let the enemy know you belong to our Lord Jesus Christ. If need be your "Higher Power" for those of you who don't believe yet! When you claim Christ Jesus, **He claims you back,** in and out of your mess. **Tempt to taste Him.** I dare you! **People,** go to Him as you are, and I promise you He will empower you to be the Kings and Queens you've been crying out to be. You don't have to cry when you know Jesus. He will drought your tears in a painful season. My God' in the counsel of Jesus He wants your mess, baggage, garbage, trash, secrets, fears, doubts, indecisiveness, hurt, health, anything threatening your wellbeing, and let's not forget the confusion in all it circulates. As His promise to me, I promise you, give it all to Jesus. Watch him workout in your favor. **Godly favor is different from your neighbor's favor. Amen...**

    I encourage you to find a place in silence, don't want to look crazy in front of anyone, find a closet in your house, send the kids to school, do it in the 3am hours. I don't care when you do it, neither does God, He just wants you to want to do it. This is what I love about people being sick and tired of being afraid. My God! **Stay with Me.** When people get tired of being scared, they become like **Jesus!** They become a God send in fear, in humility, clear of confusion in everything they were subjected. It suddenly becomes clear how to pray and **selah. I hope you didn't miss this.** Get the bookmark, **stop right here!** I feel I need to provide you with nourishment. **Here it is,** "when you're scared and your back is up against the wall, and the enemy thinks **it/he** has you cornered, because fear is present to them, I promise you the fear of God will come out of you." As the son of God risen from His tomb three days after His crucifixion, the same Holy Spirit will rise out of you against your enemies. Jesus will spring out of his anointed quick and it may be too late for your enemy. **Selah that!**

Fight Back -Or- Die for Nothing

You think it's a game, this isn't "NBA Sports," this is your life the enemy is playing with. Your life, your child's future, your children's, children future. The enemy wants your blood line to cease. You got to tell the cells of the enemy what God told me when I thought about giving up, suicide, and turning a blind eye. God said, "not today!" Today isn't your day He informed me, "I allowed you entrance in this world and I'll be the one calling you out" *My God*, this is where you leave your bookmark! *I'm prophesying to you*, this powerful truth in your hands, that's right, you' the one with fear of something. *Fear* is a gift in us all given by God before we arrived on earth. Be willing to nourish your fears to conquer your enemy." *Again, 2nd Timothy 1:7 for God does not giveth us a spirit of fear but of power and of love and sound mind.* We are so physical in this world that we're choosing to live by sight, and not faith. I don't have to see the promise of anything to know what's coming from the King of Kings. *He is already living in me,* pouring out of me the promise of each breath I take. That, there people is not science, nor some magic trick giving you breath every second of every minute, of every hour, of everyday of your life.

You so scared of your own shadow that you're trying to find ways to get rid it when you should be fighting to become one with it. *Why is this,* "wait for it" when your shadow starts going in its own direction, this means the enemy has already moved in through the flesh, by the flesh, and will finish you through an open-door policy you allowed your flesh to become. *I'm pouring out to you, right now, telling you to connect yourself to Jesus and you will never fear the shadow of your capabilities. My God!* You missed it I know you did. If you did, Try this "Jesus" is the most powerful saying you can muster out your mouth, and when you say His name, watch Him work, watch Him move mountains, and don't be premature in the days ahead, because God doesn't work for you, He's not on the clock for us, He's trying to get us to work for Him. We all have a limited time to be here. *God will be here after us.*

Surviving the Enemy

He is the Master of time and your paycheck. He's always on time. *Test that theory*, and you will learn it's not a theory, but the promise of eternal life. You can take that to church on Sunday and pay your tithing and offerings, because it is as good as done if you have Jesus is involved.

People when you got a relationship with God you got a relationship with power, and when you got that type of power in you, no one will ever mistake it, doubt it, nor come up against it unless they're ready to meet God Himself. *Nobody that knows God want to mess with His anointed. People,* your walkabout will change, your steadfast will be stern, your tone will be humble and unmistakably clear. Your strength will attract the attention of a people, and your enemies will kneel and look the other way when you walk by holding their heads down. *As a renewed person, and renewed you will be, you won't even hold a grudge against those that have wronged you. My God,* that type of renewing has God all over it. People, it's time to step into your fears and see what the real challenge of fear has on you. *So far*, fear has annihilated you from something meant to be, and you didn't even put up a fight. *It's time to put on the entire armor of God!*

In my experiences, I have put up fight's legally, physically, and mentally and lost only to leave behind an *audacity,* that I now know was the God in me. I have stepped into situations where I knew my fear was bolder than my solutions, and I would hear that big voice inside on me saying, *"What Are You Doing"* and I would say, *"I don't know, but now is not the time to be running"* and right there, in my moment of crisis I would either experience defeat, or I would experience something I couldn't dare to explain. Experience the fear and see what fear really has over you. Identify it, size up the fear, get Jesus involve in whatever plan of action involves responding to fear. *Remember when you put Jesus in it, on it, consider it already won.*

Fight Back -Or- Die for Nothing

Give fear a run for its foundation, development, or wherever it was derived and bow tie it's ugly self, return to sender with a ***Jesus stamp***. Postdate your mark. So, even after you have lived a good life, and fought the good fight, your heirs too will make the enemy run for cover. ***Make your bloodline strong against fear, in fear, so overcoming the enemy of fear isn't the challenge but a yet task.*** *People,* fear helps us respond to the enemy not run from it. The only fear to be fearful, is the fear of God and His wrath.

Surviving the Enemy

Faith Leads Us to Do Only What God Can Understand!

There comes a time in life where you absolutely must fight! There's no avoiding it, escaping it, nor hiding from it. There are fights that have absolutely nothing to do with you perhaps, or they have everything to do with you. This is where you tap into the attention of the Divine. When you step up, because it's just who you are, it gets you the attention of the Divine Sphere, the in between dimensions if you are a believer. Consciously, some of us don't believe the hereafter exist. *Yet, you are a walking example of God's miracle.* A walking testimony with the same power in you that raised Jesus from the dead. I say again, *"that isn't a magic trick that allows you to breath"* that there residing in you is the power of the Holy Spirit. Help me relay this, *please Lord*. Being born with the power of the Holy Spirit in you, raised a breathing living spirit in you. Without the power of the Holy Spirit in you brings about the outcome of a flesh with no breath, and no power of the Holy Spirit in you. It's like being still born. I said it, "a body without the spirit is "stillborn" Lord forgive me, but I got to **Selah** this truth. **People,** already - Alive in you, is a perfected gift you will need one day to discover your life purpose and your appointment(s). It is this power, the same power that raised Jesus from the TOMB that will lead you to your appointment(s). The same power that removed Daniel from the lion's den, the same power that rescued Shadrach, Meshach, and Abednego from the *fiery furnace,* and the same power that removed me from **"DC Jail"** stay with *me I'm taking you somewhere,* is the same power given to you and me at birth. That power became stronger in me as I aged and, I became more wiser to realize I had a gift in me. Why did He continuously rescue me, and even saved me from myself? I asked the epitome of my reason to be, over the years. You ready for it, *He was saving me for something much bigger than my mistakes.* God was saving me for this power in your hands right now, and so much more to follow.

Fight Back -Or- Die for Nothing

This power is greater in today than yesterday, and I'm sharing it with you right now, for you **TOO** can help save the next generations to come. *(Side Note)* the "power" of Gods appointment(s) in your life are already there waiting for you. You just have to get there by following God's promise for your life. *I promise you,* "lil James and Curtis is not going to get you to your purpose. They may even be the cause of you losing out on Gods promise. My attacks were unknown to me, but allowed by God to make it clear, He chose me *at birth* to *survive*, *teach* and *preach* this here power you hold in your hands. Live to know what God has chosen you for.

Just Live!

Surviving the Enemy
The God Fight: #1

It Comes A Time When the Universe Is Going to Challenge You to Sacrifice Without A Moment's Choice. A sacrifice declared upon you will be Relentless.

I one day I stood in front of a man to protect him, and then over top of him to prevent him from being shot and killed. **Why did I do that?** I didn't know at that time, but I just did it willingly, and unconsciously to protect him and save his life. That individual holding the gun and firing the gun at that person told me if I ever did that again they would shoot me too. I looked at them sternly, like never before, and said, "let him go" or shoot me too. ***I couldn't explain it,*** but something came out of me I was not familiar with. It was not anger but some sort of power, strength only the Lord knew. That man laid there in fear holding himself, but raise from the ground and ran to safety. ***But God*** people, ***but God.*** I don't know why I did what I did, but God puts us in positions of power, and sound mind without of being conscious of what He needs us to do, in specific moments and time. I only remember being fearless and powerful in what God physically moved me to do without question. There was no time to ask questions, only to act. ***People,*** with the power of Jesus anyone will perform. In God's chosen you've already performed the act. Would I have died for that man that night willingly and unconsciously? ***Yes!***

I definitely had a conversation with my King after this incident! Why did I do that without concern of my life? **But God People.**

Fight Back -Or- Die for Nothing

The Fight for My Soul Was On

Somebody was fighting for me. ***Me!*** We are so prized and prime growing up that the enemy is waiting and watching how we mature to temp to taste our mistakes. ***Throw some fire on that there in my "Kevin Hart" voice.*** Satan is waiting for you to slip up. ***You better be careful.*** Now, I'm sure up until that point in my life I have done everything sinful and wrong, but I knew years later from saving that guys life I had got the attention of someone very powerful in the Heavens. I find myself always looking up to the Heavens, as if waiting for someone, or something to fall from the sky for confirmation.

People, I didn't know then, that putting my life before someone else's would gain me favor in the Lord Jesus Christ. I didn't know this then, but I know it now. He has always been there for me whenever I was faced with a power greater than I am, and He's here now saying I got work to do still. When you got ***Favor in God,*** I'm sorry it's nothing nobody can do, nor say about His power and authority in, or over your life. ***Nothing!***

Surviving the Enemy

The God Fight #2

This is to all the young ladies and grown women out there in the world. I was very young when my molestation started, and I know now that my Lord and Savior was with me all along. Survival was impossible without Him. I know what you're saying, "if God was with you, why He let you get molested in the first place" **Let Me Answer with Grace**: God didn't, it was those turned blind eyes, and those addictions, and those who gave up their God given right to protect me, and you. **Distracted by fleshly pleasures.** But God made sure I didn't suffer from this recovery. **Nourish that for a minute.** We must endure something, to the be an expert in its humility. We must get past our brokenness to enhance the experience that was meant to destabilize our inner strength. When I was 6 years old, a family friend of my mom and my aunt, whom was the father of my best friend molested me. With this man I was left alone countless times, as he waited, watching, wanting to taste my youth. When I was 8 years old, it started again, my mother's boyfriend brother molested me, and continuously raped me over the years. He was yet another **babysitter**. Take heed parent(s) whom you let babysit your children. I started having sexual intercourse at 11-years old, because of the introduction of molestations in my life. I experience sex through trauma, an experience meant to be shared with my person, the person God created for me to walk about this life. Walk with me in this paragraph for no one will ever be as honest as I'm about to be with you right now. And listen well!

"Just because somebody's nastiness decided they wanted to taste and see what you felt like, doesn't give you a right not to fight, and it doesn't take away your innocence to fight back later through the power of Christ Jesus, as Vengeance belongs to the Lord now or later."

Fight Back -Or- Die for Nothing

You are as still clean as the day, hour, and minute God allowed you entrance into this world. You are still blameless in the experience of this force hood. You are still the yoke protected within your shell un-broken, as the enemy tried and failed miserably at trying to break your spirit. There's a difference between being broken and hurt feelings. You will never be BROKEN. The mistakes of the village that surrounded me didn't teach us to tell, to speak, nor was I taught good touch, bad touch to scream, and to scream on the person(s) whom ravished my flesh. *Rule #1* today: tell, go tell, tell, go tell, tell, go tell, tell, go tell, tell, go tell, tell, go tell, and tell again. Let me, *let you in on a little secret?* When you don't say anything, you give the enemy power over you every day thereafter. Every week thereafter, every month thereafter, every year thereafter. That stain of hurt grows in you from the enemy hurting you when you remain silent. *It ruins everything thereafter that's meant to blossom in your encounters and life.* But never will you be Broken. *Stay with me,* broken can't tell their story later, pain lingers and don't forget, hurt lingers don't and forget. *Let the hurt and pain heal and then BREAK your silence and the ENEMY too.* Even if it's in your timing God is always on time.

Can I speak on the *"Me Too Movement"* now, here it is years later and the world is exposing individuals not for who they are, but for committed acts in the dark when they thought no one would listen years later. *People,* proof comes from, where it comes from, it doesn't matter your authority and power today! What's done in the dark will come out in the light tomorrow. My *molester* thought he got away with what he done to me. My molester thought as the years went by, he could keep coming around thinking it would be like taking candy from a baby again, and again. *This little girl got older and my wounds got bigger.* Talking about the "Big Boom" and how it all started. Let me share how it all *Ended.*

Surviving the Enemy

People, we have got to acknowledge the pain systems we create. When I say *we,* I mean *we* as parents. When *we* turn a blind eye, when *we* think nah my friends wouldn't do that, or when our intuitions are telling us something is wrong, and *we* still do nothing. **Red light** people **"RESPOND"** to the *tell-tell* signs. Dig in the foundation that give us those feeling and yank out the roots and **Exposed the Enemy.** Back to **my molester,** thinking it would be like taking candy from a baby. He was a certified child molester primed and polished in his child molesting duties. He made a career out of it until I stopped him, and oh, did it feel **GREAT!** *True Story: This Entire Book Is True! Heaven Sent, dare you question God about it; He Was Right There with Me All Along.*

I've healed to **TELL** my story **UNAFRAID** says, "The little Girl in Me." Once upon a time there was a molester that knew my mom and her friends. I hated **Piss Place, SE. DC.,** because that's where it all started, and my mother moved to **Robinson Place, SE. DC.,** and things got better. We then moved from Robinson PL. SE, to **Pomeroy Rd. SE. DC.,** and there my molester resurfaced with that same nasty stench of how child molester now smelled to me. This was my *"trauma"* my **PTSD** I could never forget.

Pause – with Me, nobody ever knew what he was doing to me, because I never said anything, nor felt I could ever tell. The experience of being young, weak, and vulnerable has its expense people, and it shouldn't be at the expense of our innocence. *Again, remember Rule #1 today tell, go tell, tell, go tell, tell, go tell, tell, and tell again.* People, when my molester saw me sitting there all grown up, I rose like Jesus did from the tomb, *my molester* ran so fast he never looked back. *True Story! There's more but the enemy will get no glory from me, it belongs to God!*

Die for Nothing

Write Your Page of Truth Here!

Surviving the Enemy

_____...*Your Pen Is Very Powerful!*

Congratulations!
You Just Finished Writing the First Paragraph to Your Recovery Story

Fight Back -Or- Die for Nothing
Mistake #1

I never seek-ed any help. I didn't know how and didn't know who to tell. My trust had been annihilated the second I lost my innocence. I walked around bitter and angry for years, and because of this, people thought, I was just some random teenager from the projects with an attitude and issues. Never knowing I was just another victim turned *survivor.* I am now, against all odds a number above the statistics who has survive the torment. *This truth is for you.* This truth is to ensure what happened to me cease the continuation of all children being raped, molested, and murdered. Until you, me, and the rest of His chosen take a stand, it will continue to happen every day to every blind eye you turn and looks the other way. Get your child help, teach your children to say something. Teach your children good touch bad touch. Sit them down have the conversation with them over pizza and a movie. Find time to have the talks and listen to them as you expect them to listen to you. *People,* I was 18-years old when I finally told my Aunt about another family friend that was molesting me. *Family friend turned molester; blood related to my kinfolks.* Strong link to my family. *Expose them!* I told my Aunt because he too thought it was ok to come around like he did nothing wrong. *That changed that day!* Years of friendship, family-ship went right down the drain when I found the courage to speak up. So, children, teens, God's people, give somebody you trust a chance to help you expose your truth and the enemy. And if there's no one to trust *EXPOSE* them anyway. There is power in the name of Jesus. Find that fire within you to tell and tell again. *The Me-Too Movement Means It's Never Too Late.*

Surviving the Enemy
Rule #1

As Christians we're asked to do things, we never expected our conscious selves to do. **People,** I'm speaking from forgiveness. Forgive those that have hurt you. Easier thought than said. I foster it this way, because I must think about giving any part of my sentiment before doing so. It's not for me, better said than done. **No!** I must honestly think about doing this before pronouncing such gifts, as it can be mistaken for weakness. Forgiving someone doesn't mean you're weak, it's just the part of your pain you're willing to let go to heal. **Nourishment!** Pain had finally brought me to a place of forgiveness. Forgive them for they knew what they done, consciously and willingly. Here's the hard truth, **unfortunately,** they too met with a predator in their lifetime. **There I said**, yet another hard truth! **They Too!** Not the excuse of the year you want to hear, but the hard truth.

It's important for me to give you this domino effect. People are not born predators, and I'll keep it short! As children, they're introduced to unfortunate events that leaves the mark of an experience that ravages the memory of that unfortunate event, over, and over again on their souls. Victim's will become victimizers and victimizers will grow and plague what is taught. When young boys are molested this experience never leaves them. The same for young girls, it will never leave their memory bank. Just like it never left mine. There are two outcomes fight for justice now or become justice later. My justice is now, by helping others overcome the same enemy I have encountered countless times in my adolescents. Your first experience of anything is supposed to be memorable and pleasant like your first kiss, and your first pet. That first kiss leads to a wonderful kiss or a bad kiss. Whether good or bad it's up to you how you want to have victory over the enemy. Becoming a victim doesn't mean you have to stay a victim. *I choose not to be a victim, and to fight back, and fight back hard.*

Fight Back -Or- Die for Nothing
My True Story 2017

My Victory Overcoming the Molestation

Even in trying to get my life back on track the enemy wanted to make it, as hard as possible for me to achieve' what I needed to become a professional in the field, I've obtained experience through healing. Being a victim, survivor, and a parent of a victim and now survivor of the enemy challenged my recovery. Challenged my recovery by forcing me to treat a random soul with predatory behaviors, and accusation plagued against a will to recover. *The enemy was sure I would fail,* because of my vulnerabilities that stuck out of our lives like a saw dumb. Not once, but often. The enemy was sure I wasn't going to be able to successfully treat this victim/victimizer without mistreating the person that became and was predatory. *But God!* Yes, it crossed my mind to be bias, and to not treat this person, and risk exposing my vulnerable side, because someone like thee violated me, my child, and other children alike. But God!! This was a defining time, and challenge in my life to either run, and take flight, or learn from this victim now turned victimizer. I personally wanted to know, when, and why does this happen, or why do they do, what they do to children and people like you, me, and my daughter. *My God*, I learned so much, and even came to respect what the position of the opposition looks like. *Stay with me*, I learned that our faults, are not always our own initiations.

This victim turned victimizer help me heal from the molestation that had happen to me as a child. This victim turned victimizer wore two pairs of shoes and wore them well. Our sessions were so overwhelming I had to choose who to treat, and what to treat. Victim or Victimizer. I saw that wounded child within the now victimizer crying out why did this happen to me, and why do I want to hurt other children, as the monsters done to me. *Nourish that for a minute,* Nourish that! The victim loss innocents as a child, and believed there was a power to retain by repeating the same abuse over the ages on other children.

Surviving the Enemy

There was no power, it had been stolen a long time ago. While I was helping a behavior turn effectuation, I learned from this victim, turned victimizer, our actions are always ours, and owning them is a part of the healing process. *I must say,* "all my encounters led to a healing process" and a doorway to forgive those that trespassed against me. This victim allowed me wisdom to see those that trespassed against me was once innocent children, ravage by the same demonic enemy spirit that ravaged me, my daughter, and thee.

People we are not our wounds. Yet we are stagnated by what the enemy would like us to hide, forget and leave behind. Better thought about then said. It's easy to become a victim, and even easier to victimize, and even harder to experience a learned behavior over, and over again that gives the victimizers pleasure from a learned victimized behavior. I learned from this victim turned victimizer from an onset of molestation developed a ticking addiction within the flesh that needed to repeat the offending behavior. Just as an addict repeats an addiction.

Fight Back -Or- Die for Nothing

Let's Pause for A Minute.

I am in no way saying, "what this victimizer has done to other children is ok." **Hell No.** I'm saying what happened to this victim created an addiction that has no control outside of supervision, stigmatization, conditioning, and tracking. With what I've learned about the victim help me identify a deeper-rooted problem for myself, my daughter, this victim and other victims alike. I decided to treat the victim within to bring about a healing that can unlearn the predatory behavior within. I walked with the victim and encourage all victims to walk with their heads held high unashamed.

This victim turn victimizer was sent to me to break me, and make me quit my field training, by enforcing me to treat a predatory behavior that harmed me, my daughter, and other victims alike. I asked myself a question I hadn't ask myself in a long time? ***Stay with me I'm taking you somewhere with this inclination.*** I asked God what the devil was up to now! ***I Lie to You Not,*** God responded, and said, "treat the victim" and not my anger that has kept me from healing in the first place.

People I was so angry from what happened to me during my adolescence, and then years later it happened to my daughter. Being angry was just a condition currently. My anger had grown into a bitterness that had met a drought. ***Jesus!*** I was dried up in compromising forgiveness. Until I met this victim turned victimizer that helped me heal and understand a learned behavior can be a killer if untreated. This victim can head, held, high walk again and choose to be a victim no longer a victimizer. Easier thought than said. ***Please seek treatment….***

Surviving the Enemy

I thank God for giving me the opportunity to teach victimizers to unlearn what plagues them, and replace abnormal stimulus with a more acceptable or desirable potential. Hate doesn't have to bestow the world for those that didn't have a chance nor a choice. ***People, God*** exposes our wounds we cover to look normal. He wants us to heal to teach those who seem to have it all together. God is the doctor of all His wounded, and He wants His children to heal ***through power, time and Grace.*** A power we have no human understanding of how to tap into. I say to you, "help in whatever way you can to teach" and unravel the abnormality taught, and It is Gods will for everyone to recover in His light.

Not the Enemy!

Selah.

Fight Back -Or- Die for Nothing

God Fight #3

Our children, I'll keep this short, it should be long, as it's our children that needs power spoken over them. When the enemy can't get to you the cells of the enemy will go after your children. *I say again,* "when the enemy can't get to you, it will definitely go after your children." Make no mistake about the enemy's wrath against your life. When God is for you, know that the devil is going to be angry, he can't get next to you. *Remember that power I mentioned a few passages back!* While God is protecting you, you got to protect your children with that same power. *Stay with me I'm taking you through this passage.* Our children look to us the way we look to God. Our children look at us the way we once looked at our parents. They're looking for you to fix every, and anything that goes wrong in their lives.

Until you teach your children who the true living God is, your responsibility will be to show them the power of God through the miracles He performed in your life. *Parents,* when you teach your children the power of God, they will need nothing else in this world. It is you whom has the authority to pass on that power, that lives in you and now in your children. *The Holy Spirit already resides within them. It is you that must awaken the power within them!* Teach them how to access it, so in their time of need they can wield that power in all circumstances that challenge them. *My, my, my,* the reward of seeing the true living God in your children is reward enough of the true living God.

People we have work to do, so let do it. **Selah!**

Surviving the Enemy
My Fear Story: Have I Ever Had A Gun Pointed at Me

Yes! I was scared fearless because I had everything to lose. An exboyfriend drove me through an alley and pulled a gun on me. Even before this occurrence I knew I had already left the relationship. *The mind mentally processes a breakup before we're able to physically announce departure*. I didn't want to be a cover story anymore. I didn't want to be a supporter of double life situations. I, on the cover and your developed culture at night. *No!* I like the limelight, not the double life. I didn't leave a relationship due to me being unhappy, I'm the square root of unhappy, divided by sacrifices and the butterfly effects. Not because I found God. I didn't even acknowledge the power within me, that lead me, to see the **Double Life** wasn't for me. I think you missed that! Even then with a gun pointed at me, the power of God came out of me. *If that night was going to be my night, I knew it was going to be a God fight, as this cowardly spirit within the flesh I was leaving had a gun pointed at me.*

I won't put too much emphasis on this passing in my life. It was a bold purpose of the heart to experience what was to come. *Mildly* put, as any other person will learn in their lifetime. I found out he was cheating. Four years down the drain of my life. There it is again, that powerful number **#4**. I didn't at that time know, the King, my Lord and Savior stood there before me with a gun pointed at me, and I said, *"shooting me is not going to make me change my mind about staying with you."* I was scared and became fearless. If I was going to leave this world it wasn't going to be without a God fight, and I promise you God was already there, because He had plans on me writing this here power in your hands. Somebody out there in this world came before me, for me, fought for me and you, that we would at least entertain the pain we engage. *People, I had something to do with this gun being pointed at me.*

Fight Back -Or- Die for Nothing

Here we go, ***stay with me***, "I gave my heart to someone that wasn't ready to entertain the thirst my heart was yearning" God was right there protecting me, sending a God-fearing steadfast ability to speak life into an action before me. I knew even after that night, there was something in me I knew nothing about, but it was alive, well, and breathing in me! ***I'm a fighter***, and the women in my family were even stronger. There's a power we neglect, and it leaves room to fuel tiers of onsets like depression, low self-esteem, anxiety, shame, and guilt. This is not attributing to the power within you. It's filling the enemy's empty tank to reduce the power that's becoming, of the woman in you and after you. Be powerful in the lives of your daughter's and they will be powerful after you. There is power in the name of Jesus! ***That power will arise in you, just as it lives in me.***

So, Get Up and Fight!

CHAPTER SIX

Pray for The Enemy "That's Right" Pray for Them...

Again, never let the enemy confuse you being humble with being fearful. There's a great difference when God's involved. The enemy confuses you being still with being scared. *I'm afraid of God! I'm afraid of disappointing God, I'm afraid of not living my God given purpose, I'm afraid of not making Him proud.* Pray for your enemy, for no one is praying for the battle they're about to come up against. Pray for your enemy. *Why you ask?* Because they never encountered a challenge with Holy Spirit before. *They don't know why you keep getting back up after being knocked down.* They don't know why we won't give up. I'm here to tell you it's the power of Jesus inside of you. The enemy is too naive to know that God has his hands wrapped all around your persons. *Know that you are that challenge for the enemy.* If you be still for a minute, you'll learn why the enemy has chosen you to challenge. When everything looks good on the outskirt it simply means, anything not God sent wants to get in on your confetti. What the enemy doesn't know, is that your confetti are just as messy, or even messier than theirs. *People,* what we all forget sometimes is that prayer is for anybody that wants a prayer filled life. *I'm here to tell you I prayed over being fearful of responding to the enemy's wrath against my life.* Let me share my prayer for the enemy with you. As they were many against me!

But God! But God!

Fight Back -Or- Die for Nothing

A Prayer I Prayed Amid War:

Dear Father,

There are many against me and I'm just one. Father my faith is shaken and my confidence is weak. Please give me strength to steadfast against the wrath that seeks me. My response is destructive, and only awaits a fiery pit. Father, I need your strength to face the cowardice giants with confidence. Please, I beg of you I will not yield to the enemy's wrath on my life or my family's. I will not turn and run. So, if I'm your child and anointed under your covering, "let the enemy know your wrath against those that come up against my life" for it is you whom found me worthy of being saved. Let loose your mighty sword I ask of thee to armor me as you see fit. As I don't know how not to fight. Lord, the masses are against me I trust thee with all thine heart to line up the casualties that come up against me. I did, I said, "casualties, because there were many bulls bashing against my flesh and hitting what matters to me the most"

I was very afraid, and a fearful prayer brings about the power of

Jesus!

Amen/Selah…

Signed, JB, Daughter of the King…

Surviving the Enemy

Amid War "People" Pray Again

Pray for your enemy as it is those that come up against you that will need prayer. Let me tell you how faithful our God is, no matter how many times you fall, or how many mistakes you make, it doesn't matter in that light. What matters is your God life! Are you praying to the one and only true God? You have got to pray your life into an existing relationship with our Lord and Savior. The enemy kept coming, I mean it was like they had nothing else to do but come for me. I couldn't believe the attention set on me for it was orchestrated.

In the privacy of my home, I prayed, in my walking life I prayed, in my down time I prayed, and I prayed for my enemy for I knew their attacks had limitations. ***So, what did I do you ask me?*** I stood my ground with confidence. I started staring the enemy in the face for I could see who was responsible for trying to make my life less worthy. ***But God!***

The enemy was like you and me performing the likes of pure evil. ***People,*** when you discover who the enemy is, you're then able to plan how to respond to the enemy, opposite of the attacks that cometh against you. You never want to fight fire with fire. ***Never do this said-eth my criminal record.*** You see whenever someone had cometh against me and mine, I came back harder. I had to be the person not to start it but finish it. People we didn't create this earth and we're not going to be the cause of it ending. That priority belongs to God our Lord and Savior. This is not me making the statement of, "stand by and do nothing" this is me saying, ***"wait on it" "wait for it"*** and then respond with God leading, as He will see you through your circumstances. I promise, no matter the battle, the Grace of God conquers a balance only He can foresee.

Fight Back -Or- Die for Nothing

You pray for the enemy for they are only responding with their flesh. I'm almost sure they do not know what their up against when they cometh against God's anointed. Pray that God has mercy for your enemies. God's wrath for His children is made very clear. Psalm 105:15 do not touch my anointed ones; do my prophets no harm.

Pray and Selah.

JB, Daughter of the King

Surviving the Enemy
What Does It Really Take to Forgive the Enemy?

God help me explain this! People when situations arise in our lives and causes us devastation, pain, anger, despair, grief, sorrow, sadness, and even confusion, in which we all know God is not the author. Moored than likely, we choose to feel this way after someone has wronged us. ***I learned after being taught the will of God, the enemy only wins if you decide to give power to your suffering.*** People couldn't understand how I kept getting back up after being knocked down. ***But God people!*** But God. ***If the enemy didn't take your life during your knock down, get back up and steadfast, dust yourself off and move straight ahead, pass go as you've been given permission to collect Godly favor,*** as Grace has been given by the one and only true God. Stay with me I'm taking you somewhere with this here power in your hands. If you been shot and recovered, you better know what a second chance looks like. ***Hell is hot and so was that projectile the entered you.*** If you survived a terrible car accident and didn't lose your life, you better know what getting up with all your limbs feels and look like. If you survived what you know should've ended your life and you're reading this here peace of mind and power, it means you survived the enemy's plot on your life. You may not be aware, maybe you are, but you've survived something in your life up until now.

Keep surviving with God leading.

JB, Daughter of the King

Fight Back -Or - Die for Nothing

The Enemy's Plot

It means the devils plot against your life was in God's plan to rescue you, **prosper you**, cleanse you, **renew you,** and to set you apart from the rest by isolating you as God has plans for your life. **Nourish this for a minute**, if you don't forgive those that have cause you to suffer or situations that has cause you to suffer you will not prosper correctly. **My God** "what does it mean to prosper correctly"? **It means to prosper without bitterness, regret, shame, and doubt.** If God puts the vineyard in your backyard, that there is direct communication from the **Lord Himself** stating very clearly for you, **"it's your turn to prosper"** not your neighbor, not your friends, not your family but you. When it's your turn you can't take all that nasty mess with you. You can't take the suffering with you. When Jesus is involved that means power is in play people, and you've got to utilize it for the Kingdom of God and figure out how you can change what God appointed you to make a difference.

Staying focus to move ahead in the right direction means to leave all else that troubles you behind you. **Forgive** and teach what you can help rescue others from. **My momma did it,** your momma did it, God been doing it, it is written, and now **I'm about to do it for you**. Go to the vine yard, your backyard, remember only you can learn from this, and pull some fine thinly vines and twist them together "tightly" and now whip yourself into Godly shape, and get your act together. **Whip forgiveness into your walking life.** I'm going somewhere with this------☺ "people you can't forgive, because you haven't forgiven yourselves." When you've forgiven yourselves, it's like the gift that keeps on giving. **King Jesus this is delicate help me explain,** "when you've forgiven yourself the power of God reveals Himself in you." **Amen.**

Surviving the Enemy

Stay with me I'm Taking You Somewhere With this Wardrobe Change. ***Now watch them, watch you walk!*** Gone and continue your walk with the forgiveness and grace of God. This is for you reading this, I don't care what you done, I said, ***"I don't care what you done!*** "There is nothing in this world that's going to keep God from loving you. ***Nothing.*** God forgives you, now forgive yourself. What does that feel like? It's one of the most unexplainable glorified feelings in the world. When God's involve and you're dealing with the power of Jesus all I can attest to is "when you wake up in the morning and God has forgiven you and you unconsciously have forgiven yourself, you will feel the authority of the true living God in your life." Your life will never be the same I promise you.

It Will Never Be the Same!

Selah.

Fight Back -Or- Die for Nothing

Hatred vs. Heart

True Testimony!

As I set there in **DC Jail** kneeled on the cold floors. I pleaded with God to look into my heart and find the truth as I didn't do what I have been accused. I wept and cried for days, weeks until God responded. *My God,* when the Lord responds people, it becomes the only revelation that stains the soul of question do our God really lives. He heard me and held my heart in His Hands, and saw my iniquities, the truth, nothing but the truth so helps us all who dare to lie to the true living God. I learned after my release from jail why God revealed Himself to me. Mathew 5:8 Blessed are the pure in heart, for they shall see God. If you know me personally you have heard my testimony. If you're reading this power in your hands then you've heard me mention God revealing Himself to me in Jail. People, after meeting my Lord and Savior in the flesh, no one could sale me nothing to trick me into denying my King. **Nothing!** Even more signifying, God found me worthy, pure in heart, and it's nothing man can do to change that. When God is for you, who can be against you. Validation is all those I've assisted, saved, and helped without thinking throughout my life. *You see,* when God looks into your heart, the years of your life will speak all truth. People, when you ask God to do something *"won't He do it"* won't He do it? *Yes,* He will & did it for me! That's why I'm able to will to you this power in your hands. The heart is where Jesus is, in us, as we're in Him. So, what does the heart do against hatred, what does it do for us when speaking of love and hatred, hatred crushes everything we know as a unity.

Love makes it all make sense.
JB, Daughter of the King…

Surviving the Enemy
The Love of God Conquers All.

If we weren't too busy giving love and affection to fast cars, pricey shoes, clothes, and the root of all evil, like a squirrel chasing a nut half of our life's purpose would be fulfilled already. It's a difference between chasing those corns and being scorned for them. *Come on, stay with me, I'm taking you somewhere.* These are the very things you have been tempted to killed for, robbed for, threaten for, betray for, and shamed for, and even sell your soul for. *Ok, pause,* you didn't shoot lil James over those $200.00 yeezy's, and you didn't car jack the lady at the gas station. *So, you say!* But I bet you know somebody, that know somebody, that did. *People,* we are loving and hating over all the wrong things. If you find yourself'' too hating and loving anyone over anything, other than what God has put forth in humanity, you have left the indeed plans God has for your life.

God is in the heart people. It's the doorway, and He is watching what you do whole heartedly from your heart without thinking. There is good and evil in us all, and hatred has nothing to with this. Being good is easy, being bad is with and without conscious intentions. *Our emotions lead us to unconscious thinking and then actions.* Hating someone comes with premeditated intentions to do something out of the nature of cause and effect by emotional damage. Just thinking of being hateful is planting destruction in the heart where God lives in us. *Wait for it, wait for it,* if God is in our hearts, and you bring hatred in the heart where He lives, God's going to leave that toxic place by your own dismissal. *People when God is no longer present in the heart you will know it, and feel that something has went terribly wrong.* It's like a part of you dying or losing someone close to you that's no longer here. You don't want that trust me I know. *God knows that things happen.* God knows that evil approaches us every day of our lives the moment we leave our sacred places.

Fight Back Die for Nothing

As I mentioned in earlier chapters the power of the enemy wins when we don't have faith in our prayers, and faith in our relationship with God or your higher power. People, the heart is a sacred place and you just can't hand it to anybody, or everyone. You must protect your God sacred places, and the heart is where Jesus our Lord and Savior lives. ***So, don't just go around giving your heart away.***

Surviving the Enemy

By Example!

Giving away your heart is like relinquishing Jesus from your way of living as we all get a little detoured, but it shouldn't be at the cost of your relationship with God. God is watching you, and He's like, "have you lost your mind" you traded me for some yeezy's. When it's too late, and Craig, and Kee-Kee has taken your heart, drained it of all its Godly favor, and God given talents, you then will notice somethings just not the same without Jesus. You better get you some, New Balances and walk well. God show me the way the devil's trying to shut me down. *Jesus walks with me,* with me. *Let me stop I don't want no trouble from Kanye W.*

You will be back at the heart of Christ, our Lord and Savior, the one you come to know of many chances, all snotty nose, and wanting to get back in His good grace. And as the God of all promises, He will be there to renew you in all the ways He destined you to be, because that's just how God operates in His children. God may not dwell where hatred is, but when hatred is through with you, God will be there to redeem you in whatever condition hatred has left you, and that's what our God, your God, and a higher power does. You must come to know' it's normal to get upset, emotional, angry, bitter and even jealous, but when you allow these un-Godly conditions to turn into hatred it leads you to think, and conjure hatred for your fellow brothers, sisters, neighbors, spouses, and against your families. By this consumption you have removed a hedge of protection more powerful than your enemy could ever bring forth over your life.

You better try those "New Balances" and walk well. Jesus, walks, with me, with me, with me.

Fight Back -Or- Die for Nothing

People, the devil wants what no man can put under, and that's what God Giveth rather it be favor, grace, mercy, protection, power, oil, soil, the vine yard, blessings, and most importantly an abundance to fuel your bloodline. ***Be aware,*** know that this is what we take on, in our lives, passing this stigmatization down to our children leading them to spread hatred, or love in this world. Choose wisely what you mode into your children, and how you guide your children down the path of righteousness they're to harvest from. You bear this responsibility until they are fruitful and ready to be release from the vineyard in the backyard. It was your parents' responsibility for you, and it will be your responsibility for yours.

Now if you weren't raised this way, let me apologize for whatever mishaps that have bestowed you in your childhood. Let me apologize for the foes that have cometh against you without corrections. Nobody apologized to me either. So, "I'm terribly sorry if you suffered, and encountered repeated behaviors of your parental past." I really, really am, but today it's up to you to do things differently, not better, but different than how you were raised. I promise you, if you don't do things differently, the hatred of your past will befall you and yours, and their bloodlines to come. Be that change for your children, and their children's, children future. Be the Change that breaks generational curses. ***Make It Right!*** You have a Godly parental responsibility to Make It Right!

By God Make It Right!

Surviving the Enemy

True Story!

In the words of a mourning parent: I buried my oldest son in 1996, my middle son in 2006, and my youngest boy in 2016.

These are the words of someone you know. Someone you grew up with. Someone you were in a relationship with. Someone you gave birth to and someone's father, brother, uncle, cousin, and friend. *So, I ask you where does it stop?* Where do we end this senseless pattern of pray, target, and pretargeted? Why do I say pre-targeted? When you lose one, and another and another until you have nothing else, it means somewhere along the lines, you removed that God-fearing armor, you stop praying and protecting your bloodline. *You stop including Jesus in your worries and fears.* People I'm here to tell you what you're not ready to accept, *"you gave up your God fight"* that's right, you gave up your *God fight.* Let me be of the spirit of wisdom and self-expose, *"I have lost to the likes of evil through hatred for my enemy."* Let me say this again, *"I have lost to the likes of evil through hatred for my enemy."* I have lost countless times against the enemy, but it came a time to realize you and I can only lose something, or someone if we gave up a long time ago. *Control your emotions I'm going somewhere with this,* if you lose hope and forget faith, how is what important to you protected? This is not to say something wouldn't have happen, this is to say maybe it would've, could've happen differently. *The love of God through Jesus from the heart conquers all hatred.* Ask me How? *I can't wait to tell you!* When you receive it, it's like a, "**Jesus Seasoning**" **hmmmmm** Good. **True Story**

In the words of FORGIVENESS: when one can FREELY, forgive from the heart the person that has taken life away from them "it was a GOD LOVE that produced a Deeper-rooted forgiveness to heal a life for a life of pain. Every Day We Forgive! We Have to Forgive People. If we don't, we die inside leaving the power of God in us faithless and lost forever.

CHAPTER SEVEN
Give God the Glory

Glory belongs to nobody, but King Jesus in all things overcome and steadfast. Praise Him the way you praise your new car. Praise Him when you get that new job. Give God the glory as He heard your prayers and answered them. Give God the glory for the favor He has placed upon your life, your children's life, your family and friends. Give God the glory as He's given breath in the morning to awaken you and beauty for ashes upon night fall. Give God the glory for your good health, renewing it and curing you from what you thought would overtake you. Give God the glory for sending you a spouse that has born children with you. Give God the glory for being faithful when all else has failed. Give God the glory for being there for you when your human dependencies abandon you. Give God the glory for renewing your confidence. Give God the glory for finding you worthy of a second chance. Give God the glory for keeping you safe. Give God the glory for bringing your children into this world. Give God the glory as He found you worthy to be saved and gave His only son for our sins and humanity. Give God the Glory for guiding your steps when you got lost in the wilderness. Give God the glory for allowing you to be found down by the wayside. Give God the glory for allowing our faith to yearn for more of His Unconditional love. Give God the glory as He's the reason why you're reading the powerful truth. Give God the glory as He's your provider, protector, keeper, redeemer, and promise keeper. Give God the glory as He would never forsake you. Give God the glory as He is the creator of all things, and know our inner darkest secrets, wants, worries, fears, and addictions. Give God the glory as He's the beauty in our hearts, and the attraction that draws our attention to heavenly factors over earthly qualities. Give God the glory as He's the gift giver of life for those of us that suffer from child barren.

Surviving the Enemy

Give God the glory as He appoints those forgotten and appoints those that have been deemed unworthy. Give God the glory as what's done in the dark will come into the light. Give God the glory for your enemies will lose their way plotting against you. Give God the glory as He will restore what was lost and stolen. Give God the glory as He will bring your enemy to be kind. Give God the glory for when He anoints you, it would be foolish for anyone to come up against you. Give God the glory as He will bestow upon you what looks impossible. Give God the glory as He will empower you to be successful in all that challenges you. Give God the glory as He's given you the authority to walk in His ways, and spread His will as He finds you exceptional to teach. Give God the glory for He has chosen you over earthly powers to shine your light through the darkness most of us can't see through. Give God the glory as He loves us so much, He sacrificed His only son for humanity, a humanity we don't appreciate, a humanity we walk in called earth. Give God the Glory as the humanity we come to see as life in a dark place God gives us light to find Him. In return, He only ask that we love each other and continue to multiply to make up a human face the devil wants to cease.

Give God the glory!

Fight Back -Or- Die for Nothing

Victory Already Written in Gods Promises Through (Jesus)

Let's start with what's written already. God never lied to us, humans did. Nowhere in the NKJV of the Holy Bible does God say to trust human beings. The first lesson here is to leave trusting to God. Trust God and the right people or at least those appointed will do God's bidding in guiding your steps. For those of you that know the "Ten Commandments" let this be a teaching for the unknown.

1st Commandment, I am the Lord thy God, which have brought thee out of the land of Egypt, out of the house of bondage. "God's tells us here and now It was He that has rescued us from what held us captive. 2nd Commandment make no mistake "Thou shalt have no other gods before Him" Don't Do it!!3rd Commandment, Thou, shalt not take the name of the Lord thy God in vain. 4th Commandment Remember the sabbath day, to keep it holy. My God "He only ask That thee keep it Holy people." 5th Commandment, Honor thy mother and father no matter what! People it's never too late to heal. 6th Commandment, Thou, shalt not kill!!!! **My God** it is written people. I'll touch a little more on this later in this chapter. 7th Commandment, Thou, shalt not commit adultery. Simple! 8th Commandment, Thou, shalt not steal. Plenty of repentance for this one. God Forgives all the time. 9th Commandment, Thou, shalt not bear false witness against thy neighbor. Woe, Woe, and Woe. 10th Commandment, Thou, shalt not covet neighbor's house, wife, animals, or anything else.

God saideth "You shall set up these stones, which I command you today on mount Gerizim" People, I'm telling you to set them high in your hearts and your home. I'm telling you to set them high in places where you're trying to go, and attributes achieved for the kingdom of the highest God. God gave us these written victories and asked us to apply them in our lives for victory was already written.

Surviving the Enemy

Simply following and applying these commandments are the promises of the true living God. **People**, you are already victorious in your walking life. All you must do is look at your every waking moment and thank God for it is He whom will do the rest throughout your day, and throughout your life. Just put Him before and above all things, and you will live victorious in every promise of God.

This people are written in the NKJV HOLY BIBLE.

Selah!

Fight Back -Or- Die for Nothing
Ten Scriptures God Promises You!
"Jesus"

2nd Peter 1:4 And because of His glory and excellence, He has given us great and precious promises. These are the promise that enable you to share His divine nature and escape the world's corruption caused by human desires.

Jeremiah 29:11 For I know the plans I have for you," says the Lord. "They are pans for good and not for disaster, to give you a future and a hope.

Mathew 11: 28-29 "Come to me, all you who are weary and burdened, and I will give you rest. Take my yoke upon you and learn from me, for I am gentle and humble in the heart, and you will find rest for your souls."

Isaiah 40: 29-31 He gives power to the weak and strength to the powerless. Even youths will become weak and tired, and young men will fall in exhaustion. But those who trust in the Lord will find new strength. They will soar high on wings like eagles. They will run and not grow weary. They will walk and not faint.

Philippians 4:19 And this same God who takes care of me will supply all your needs from His gracious riches, which have been given to us in Christ Jesus.

Romans 8:37-39 No, despite all these things, overwhelming victory is ours through Christ, who loved us.

Proverbs 1:33 But all who listens to me will live in peace, untroubled by fear of harm.

Surviving the Enemy

John 14:27 "I am leaving you with a gift-peace of mind and heart. And the peace I give is a gift the world cannot give. So, don't be troubled or afraid.

Romans 10:9 If you confess with your mouth that Jesus is Lord and believe in your heart that God raised Him from the dead, you will be saved.

Romans 6:23 For the wages of sin is death, but the gift of God is eternal life through Christ Jesus our Lord.

People allow these promises of God to lead your hearts into an unwavering faith, hope, as an unseen power will capture every prayer believed that our King lives forever in us.

Selah!

Fight Back -Or- Die for Nothing

What Does it Mean to Leave the Battle to God?

People misunderstand this statement all the time. God didn't say stand there and let Satan have his way with you, and yours. *No,* God didn't say let your neighbor have his way with your wife. *No!* God didn't say let your children run wide without scourging them. *No!* God didn't say turn your back on life's problems, and challenges. *No!* God didn't say give up and lie down. *No!* And I'm not telling you that. God said put Him before all your battles and let Him lead you into victory as the battle is His. The war to come is the spiritual warfare, we come to know through the power of prayer, faith, hope, and God fearing. *My God*, people, we're not alone, and we can't continue to walk this earth God created for us to dwell, and act like we don't even know His power, worthiness, love and sacrifices for our sins. When He say the battle is His, that's just what He means! *Wait a minute, listen,* "He has given His only son for our earthly sins." *Do you get it,* "no human is willing to sacrifice their children for another, or for the greater good, willingly! Let's be honest, let's be honest! We treat our children like our property, like they're all we got, and yet, forget that God is the gift giver of our children, but gave His son for our sins. To say we know God, is to say, "honestly, nothing in this world means anything to me if I ain't got King Jesus reigning over my life." People our children look to us like were God, and we look to our Heavenly Father, at least those of us that know better than to fix everything that hurts or hinder us ourselves. News flash people, you got to be willing to put the King, our God before every and anything in your life. Never mistake what He appoints you to do for His Kingdom and, as a people.

Surviving the Enemy

Put God first, and that means God comes before your children, mother, father, family, money the root of all evil, house, cars, fancy stuff, travel, business plans, achievements, and anything you can think of that pleases you, should not come before King Jesus. People, we do it every day, and our God is hurt, because after all He has sacrifice for us, we can't put away our fleshly needs to put him first. That's all He wants from us; is to show Him we appreciate His sacrifice to procreate for our souls to live an earthly eternal life amongst each other in peace. People I promise you just as God promises me if you surrender all you are to the Lord and Savior, all that you are will be magnified by the Kingdom, the Father, and the Son. If it feels you're alone, people that's the works of our enemy. You're never alone when you put Jesus first. You're never alone in no battle when the Holy Spirit lives in you. My God people when the Holy spirit rest in you there's nothing no one can do to crush you. Yes, the enemy will cause you problems, headache, lost, despair, but with the power of Jesus, our Lord and Savior the Holy Spirit within you, I promise you, you will rise like you've never been touch. That alone is the promise of Jesus. People Jesus conquered the world after His death. Blessed are those that believe in the blood of Jesus Christ, for everything you want to prosper. ***He will bless you and your house for stead fasting in Him.***

Selah.

Fight Back -Or- Die for Nothing

To put God first is to accept the Lord Jesus Christ into your hearts, home, challenges, problems, fears, worries, finances, prayers, tithings and offers, trials and tribulations. You must be willing to receive Jesus, to share how decisions made with the Holy Spirit are the best decisions made for your families, and friends when facing the enemy. Why is it imperative we do it this way? **Because the battles are God's and His alone before you take your family and friends through Hell and back.** He will see to it that your enemies know your name, because you cried out to Him. He will make sure your problems are now His, just as you're His child. Your enemies will know just how much God loves you when they, or whatever comes up against you.

Selah.

Surviving the Enemy

How Do You Know If God Lives in You – Or – Not?

Write It Down! How Do You Know?

_____
_____
_____
_____
_____
_____
_____
_____
_____
_____
_____
_____
_____
_____
_____
_____
_____
_____
_____
_____

_____. *And this is how I know! Selah His Promise…*

Chapter Eight
How A Single Human Being Can Save Just One

Every day is a chance one can go out in the world, and provide kindness to someone, or anyone. It can also be a chance that we can intentionally save a life. Let me tell you why I said intentionally. Intentionally means you already know the person whose life you're going to sacrifice for today. You already made up in your mind, you're going to change this person's life just because you want to make a difference. *My God* when we wake up like this with these intentions it pleases our King Jesus. Out the window with the notion of being willing because someone else might see or notice what you're doing. So what, God said, "today do it in front of the world" for the world to see what I awaken in you to do every day. Teach them to show and bestow kindness for the world to see, "how not to turn a blind eye." Be a showoff today. Show the world what they're supposed to be doing for the kingdom and for humankind. Be a charity for a lost cause, and remember what we have lost and give life to it once more.

People, being A people, for the people, by the people brings us together for the greater good of this nation. On this day of greatness for you, don't filter as God saideth, "the unchosen were welcome to celebrate in His name," and all His children good, and those marked as bad, black sheep, cast out, banished, shamed, lied on, abandoned, ignored, and the forgotten are good. God saideth, "on this day come one, come all and be saved." Our Lord and Savior awaits the day for one race and cease separation in the physical realm we walk. This is the reality God created for humankind not separation for yours and mine to dwell in our walk of life. There are no differences in Christ, we are all His children, and it's our Godly responsibilities to take notice how were so much alike. We display hate against one another for our differences. My King chose me to write this piece of power you're holding. He chose me at birth, set apart from others to be different to survive the multitude of attacks mentioned and some unspoken.

Surviving the Enemy

At a very young age He knew I was leader. I had to trust God to lead me through the warfare my ancestors, and my family before me, whom had to battle in a realm where discernment knew no boundaries. **Not only, was I not popular as a child**, but I wasn't popular in school, but notoriety had found me through my flesh, and attracted me all friends of the flesh. Again, the physical things in this world that bring us pleasure will also bring you problems that make you call on Jesus. That type of pleasure brought the attention of thirsty souls alike. Thirsty to get high, drink, immoral behaviors, and deceitfulness of fellow friends and reputations. You are what you hang with, it's the saying of the year. I decided some time ago I wanted more. So much more; I wanted real friends, not just friends I could care about, correct, and be honest with, but I wanted the type of friends that wasn't afraid to check my box either.

God chose me to be the narrator of this work to lead, and to be a light in the lives of those I've came across. Rather it be by passing, bus stop, grocery shopping, church, neighboring, or family functions. I made sure to engage in the open-door invitations in the moment. I was always different, and being different sometimes can lead people to believe you're stupid and dumb, but I knew something in my heart could never hold a grudge, because I found caring, sharing, and the love in my heart to be my biggest assets beside God. I found the love of God a long time ago, because I yearned for it, and God filled my heart with joy and kindness, regardless of the evil that tried to make me feel different. Obviously, this didn't always go well, but I was never alone with my open heart. I always brought strangers home to heal, help, and befriend. I always brought stray animals' home, and between the strangers and strays I literally drove my mother crazy. **Laughs just thinking about it!** Even at a young age my heart was designed to care and extend kindness in this world that God planted in me at birth.

Fight Back – Or- Die for Nothing

My openness has led me to get hurt, betrayed even, but the door way to Jesus is the heart and if the heart says to show kindness, this is what our King is asking us to do. *For me*, it felt good being a good friend, and even a good listener at such a young age.

You will come to notice you have these habits, and for the life of you, you can't understand why every time you do good, somebody treats you bad. I mean, it's probably become a serious issue for you by now, and you seriously want to start treating people like they treat you. That's, that, give them a taste of their own medicine mentality, or that, "you going to need me again," and I won't be there for you." *People*, this is, what happens when we continuously misplace our God given gifts. *OMG*, if God has placed kindness in you at birth to share it with the world to harvest the persecution of abusive friends, family, and foes; I say to you, "do you know how blessed you are?" Do you know what you have been charged with to do and conquer? Let me tell you this, "God has bestowed kindness in you, and me to be overcomers of abuse." *Stay with me*, I'm leading you in the righteous way of kindness. That same kindness your friends, family, and foes took advantage, is the same kindness God knew you were going to need to forgive the enemy for what they have done to you. God knew you were going to need this kindness to be humble when you do overcome, and *win, win, win, win.* That kindness is leading you to your breakthrough as an overcomer, and a victor. That same kindness is in you right now, to teach those coming behind you, kindness will rule tomorrow.

As an adolescent growing up, I had this God habit of wanting to fix people to my liking, or what they needed to be. *Talk about build a bear,* but I found myself wanting to fix what was broken and what was sad in people. Anything I sensed was wrong, or looked wrong I wanted to fix them. That was just the God in me to change what I sensed was broken.

Surviving the Enemy

During this stage in my life I learned I was a sensitive, and could sense almost anything if it was crying out from within. My plague I called it, but I've matured and realized, it was yet another gift from God. As I aged, **stay with me,** I ordered myself a natural boss over those I cared about. This didn't always come across as receptive, even though, I always knew what was best, and always knew when something wasn't right for the people I loved and cared dearly for. Being one's, savior is a blessing, and an appointed job in the Kingdom of God. This maybe you appointed to watch over your entire family, and no one knew this but you and God. Have you ever found yourself saying, "why doesn't no one listen" after the big boom that impacted everybody and could've been prevented? It's ok, pat yourself on the back, and maybe, just maybe someone with a little bit of wisdom may say, "I think it's time we listen." **Remember to stay humble.**

God had chosen me before my birth, to bestow gifts, He found would be helpful in reaching humankind. Yes, "I have saved people" help solved cases, and even warned people that took heed, and even some that didn't want to know. My gifts over the years has led me to know myself better, and the people I encountered that will never understand the power of God, not alone Jesus really is in me. It's ok, to be different, don't expect the world to except you, just find ways to save just one with the gifts God has bestowed in you, and God will make you a light in this world. Here's a little secret for the gifted, don't tell everyone what you're capable of doing. It's a one-way ticket to see a **shrink.** Hold sacred what God has given to you at birth, and save those you can, and they will come to love and appreciate you for who you are. We're very special creatures and can easily be mistaken for the enemy. Go and plant yourself in whatever field you've chosen for yourselves, and spread all that is good about you, as our Lord and Savior has blessed you, for others can see a great harvest sprout out of you.

Fight Back -Or-Die for Nothing

As you and I are His children and planted in good dirt to bear the fruits of this world. ***It is now time to show the enemy the harvest of your past.***

Show how God led you through.

Selah.

Surviving the Enemy
God's Kindness Without Strings Attached

God has done everything for mankind with no strings attached. Not one little stitch held in place to save this world. Not one stitch! God created this earth for us to live and promised not to destroy it again. ***Genesis 9:11 I established my covenant with: Never again will all life be cut off by the waters of a flood; never again will there be a flood to destroy the earth.*** " I have set my rainbow in the clouds, and it will the sign of the covenant between me and earth. Our God, your higher power sacrificed His only son Jesus, because He believed we would one day overcome all sin. I'm saying to you, ***"A people, go and be like God, and do something for nothing with no strings attached.*** We've become so attached to the physicality of this world; it wants something from you in return. God asked only that we love one another. We have absolutely forgot about God and His mercy, not alone His kindness He's bestowed upon us in our undeserving ways. We've become accustom to survive without God, and somehow forgot He is still the foundation we walk on. We **Heavenly** sleep and live in our safe customs without giving to God in return. ***Go ahead be offended and defend yourself against God I dare you.*** I haven't always given without looking for something in return" I was comfortable with give and take.

I was comfortable with taking and not giving properly in return. I was comfortable with getting over on others if I came out on the better end. Until one day I got a taste of that medicine having to give without receiving. I learned what it really felt like to give, lose, and be left behind. I didn't like it then, and I didn't like the lesson learned about myself as a child of God. I came to realize I didn't have to take from nobody, because I already had moored than enough to survive, walk, talk, and live like the daughter of the King. Today I have moored than enough to walk, talk, and live as our Father see fit. There's nothing in this world that can stop what God has for you. So, just give without fear of being left empty.

Fight Back -Or- Die for Nothing

God has put it on my heart to tell you today, you have enough to live accordingly, and to give to your family, the homeless, charities, churches, and those that have lost. Give until it hurts you to give no more, not your all, but no more. Put this on your hearts people, and your souls to teach one, each one to give with no strings attached. Give to the schools, colleges, and I plead with all gift givers help those that can't afford to go to college attend college. Make someone's dreams come true today. Go do it right now! Be a people to change the world, be a people to help someone fix their debt. Help someone you don't know. Let it be a stranger for true kindness to have no name, as God pleaded it to be this way in humanity.

Surviving the Enemy

God Wants to Know, "Are You're an Organ Donor"

Give Life!

Donate life, that's right, ***"no I'm not crazy,"*** I know my Father the true King, and now it's your turn to get to know Him. Do your driver's license or non-drivers ID say "donor" in the event God calls you home? ***Not yet,*** but just in case, does it say, "you were humanly ready" to give life people. Kindness is moored than holding the door for your follower, or the person before you, Kindness is in the heart and it's free, and so is the kingdom, we call it favor. ***Say it with me, "Favor"*** God will give it in abundance for your small kind gestures. Giving a stranger a hug and telling them it's going to be ok. Standing up for someone and taking a hit for them is the grandstand of a leaping unconscious heart. Canceling a big trip to spend it with children less fortunate is the kindness this world requests. Spending your bonus on a less fortunate child for the holidays doesn't earn you favor in the human world; it earns you the love of A human race and gives hopes to a child of God. That's how you perform with no strings attached. You do get something from all this? ***You get to meet the God in you.***

Hi, it's nice to meet you.

I'm JB, Daughter of the King.

Fight Back -Or- Die for Nothing
How to be A Part of Something Bigger Than Yourself

First, I would like to give a **Godly Thank You** to those that are already serving in a bigger capacity pass themselves. I would like to thank our **Police Officers** for serving and protecting this country in the best of their ability and their expected responsibility. Thank you so very much. ***Secondly,*** I would like to thank all **Fire Fighters** that put their lives on the line racing into fiery furnaces, and lion's dens every day to save lives like mine. I want to give a special thanks to the 9, 000 that continued to fight a relentless California fire. Thank you for your tireless fight against only what you know how to handle with God leading. Thank you to **EMT workers** for your fast response in our need of help. I was very thankful every time you were there for my mom. ***Every time!*** Thank you for keeping many alert ensuring a safe arrival to the hands be of **God**, or the **Doctors.** I know of the stories of the many **EMT's** lost in the line of duty. Thank you in the powers that be. Thank you to a very special group of people. Our **911 dispatchers** rather it be police, fire, or ambulance. Your job is intense, and important as you ensure us *(a people)* that help is on the way. I don't know where we would be as a people if you didn't exist. You're a connecting doorway to the world of help, and I thank you from my Godly heart. You are welcomed, appreciated, needed, and most importantly a special part of this world. ***Thank you*** so very much. ***Thirdly,*** and not least the **US Army, Military, Marines**, and other forces that fight for this country, thank you for keeping us safe. Thank you for your sacrifice, thank you for **willingly** stead fasting against the enemy. This country, or no medal, can ever thank you enough for your sacrifice, but **God our Lord and Savior** couldn't have chosen a better nation for you to protect. God makes no mistake in those He chooses to lead (a people,) and to lead this country. ***Lastly***, and not least, His perfected chosen leading countless to lead, and a chance to be a part of greatness now, and a bigger history than ourselves in the future.

Surviving the Enemy

God appointed **Counselors, Deacons, Deaconess, Doctors, Guardians, Parents, Pastors, Preachers, Prophets, Prophetess,** Protectors**, Teachers, Therapists, Shepard's, and Heavenly Angels.** All one village to proceed in the body of Christ.

God shaped our hearts into His expectation. I don't know about you, but every agent or agency above has played a part in my life and is the reason, besides God I'm still alive today. These people make up 40% of unconditional regard for humanity. The other 60% is up to us, as a people to trust God, and be willing to do our part to better this nation, and to steadfast in our humanity for a greater good. I can't be the only human that wants to live abundantly as God's promise on this earth before we get to Heaven. If our best is good enough for God. Is your best really your best for God? **This is not a dream** people. **9/11** was real, humans were lost forever, and the pain is still real all year around with 911 now a national day of remembrance. The lost was great, and every single entity mentioned above came to the rescue of souls lost, and survivors that live to tell their story of survival. Under fire, God instilled in us the power to act just like Him without question.

This day **9/11** marks history of an attack on mankind and humanity. This is why, **as a people**, we can't stain the hearts of each other with murder, mayhem, and strife taking each other out, for meaningless nothings. **Nothing worth ending your tomorrow over.** We will get there as a people, and I promise, as God promises, you will be a part of a greater good which is bigger than yourselves. You all have your parts to fulfill. Awaken your hearts and ask someone, "where you can help today."

Selah That!

Fight Back -Or- Die for Nothing
How Can You Be A Part of Something Bigger Than Yourselves?

Surviving the Enemy

_____
_____
_____
_____
_____
_____
_____
_____
_____
_____
_____
_____
_____
_____
_____
_____
_____
_____
_____
_____. *Consider It Done God! I Will pursue it to the end.*

This Is Your Promise to Our God! The Pen Is Very Powerful!

CHAPTER NINE
"People, God Doesn't Know How Not to Fight for His Children"

I say this with conviction, *"God doesn't know how not to fight for His children."* I know for a fact my Father conquers all that comes up against me. No matter the enemy, no matter my giant, no matter the weapon the formed against me, my God, our God, your god, your higher power doesn't know how not to conquer what comes up against His children. **Especially His anointed.** People sometimes ask, "does God get angry?" *Yes*, he gets very angry when his children are threatened, when His children, are persecuted senselessly, and when the enemy come up against His children. It would be like coming up against God Himself. When God, the power of our Lord and Savior Jesus reigns in your fight, I promise you, as you may think you're standing there all alone, the Holy Spirit will awaken in you, and then out of you He will reign, and your enemy will know nothing about whom their up against. Forgive me for boasting, "I'm testifying to His promise over my life" and to those that trust Him over all your problems, challenges and **God fights.**

Sarah Young wrote on this day in 2004, 15th November in "Calling Jesus" Approach problems with a light touch. *My God!* As mortals for the most part, this is hard to tackle, because were so hardheaded and need to be felt. She went on to say, *"When your mind moves towards a problem area, you tend to focus on that situation so intensely that you lose sight of God!"* My God, *omg* again. People think about it, pause for a second, if we did everything with God leading us in our mistakes, there would be less conflict and many more victories. She goes on to say, "in light of God you put yourself against difficulties as if you had to conquer it immediately." People, people, people. God goes on to tell her to tell us, *"our mind is already geared up for battle, and our bodies become tense and anxious."* I kid you not, she goes on to say, *"unless we achieve total victory, we feel defeated."*

Surviving the Enemy

This is exactly how we respond as Humans. This is proof people, the battle belongs to our Lord, and there is no victory without Him leading you. There's self-destruction your way, and then there's victory God's way. **What Way, God's Way, The Only Way!!!!**

There's more, Sarah goes on to say, "God tells us in, *"Jesus Calling"* there is a better way." When a problem starts to overwhelm your thoughts, she says, "God said' **bring your problem to Him and talk to Him about it and look at it in the Light of His Presence.** Do you know what it feels like to be in the presence of the King? *"I Do!"* God will put some much-needed space between you, and your concerns enabling you to see from His promise your concerns are *lightweight* to His mighty hand. You will be surprise at the results. Sometimes you may even laugh at yourself for being so serious about something so significant. You will always face problems in your life. More importantly, you will always have God with you helping you to handle whatever you encounter.

Approach problems with a light touch by viewing them in Gods revealing Light. And as God promises you'll be surprise at the outcome, and again laugh for taking yourself so seriously. **Thank you**, Sarah Young, as page 334 was a light in my darkness not alone your entire book *Jesus Calling*. Again, people God didn't say not to steadfast He said to approach your problems with Him leading. He will never leave you alone. You may look alone; the enemy may think you're alone, but in you lays the power of Jesus the same power that raised Jesus from the tomb is the same power that gives us breath to awaken in the morning, as well as the same when night befalls us. That's Gods promise in the morning and God's promise every night. If there ever was a time, you knew you wasn't alone, then you're aware it was a power far greater than yours, that you survived and came out problem solved. But **God People. Selah.**

Fight Back -Or- Die for Nothing
When God Waits on You (WOW) – Please Pay Attention Here!!!!!

There comes a time when you want what you want, and when you want it! There comes a time when doing things your way seems the only way possible to you. There comes a time when you keep telling yourself you're right over, and over again. There comes a time when you know exactly what you're doing wrong, and just don't give a rat's tail. *Well guess what?* God knows exactly what you're doing, and how long you've been doing your deeds. He also, knows getting through to you is like the temperament of a brick wall. *But thank God He's into rebuilding!* Amen. God as I know Him will tear you down just to put you back together again! *That's how much the KING of Kings loves you.* You forgot our God move mountains, and will chase you down until you change your ways if He finds you worthy to be saved. Our Father is in the business of saving people, and even saving you from you. You ever wonder why the same thing keeps happening to you every few years or so, or have you notice a pattern of behaviors' where you just can't get right. It's called our inner most determination in doing it our way. *But God people.* He will eventually have his way with us. Not because we don't have a choice. *Stay with me I'm going somewhere this.*

It's because we were given purpose at birth and somehow between spiritual warfare, and the world we live in called humanity we got lost in the physicality of our purposes. *What we see, touch, and engage leads us away from our spiritual duties.* Sometimes we don't learn what those duties are until a lifetime passes us by. *What a shame!* I'm forty-two years old and at every decade of my life up until now, I received a visit from my Father informing me my duties await me. *For some reason His visits are more frequent!* Scared unknowingly what my duties were, I was fulfilling them over the years of my life. Godly duties have nothing do with having a job and going the church and paying your tithings and offerings.

Surviving the Enemy

These are the responsibilities of all people in the way of our Lord. *No,* it's much more gratifying than our physical world. I'll share it, let's start with what is written:

Joel 2:28

"And it shall come to pass afterwards, that I will pour out my spirit on all flesh; your sons and your daughters shall prophesy, your old men shall dream dreams, and your young men shall see visions. **Some of us have duties to prophesy in this life.**

> *I have my dreams and visions unashamed to share what God has given me to bestow upon this world. Yes, I am different! Yes, I can foresee when the world means me harm, but I'm Glad my Father the King is the creator of it all and my protector.*

Numbers 12:6

And He said, "Hear my words: If there is a prophet among you, I the Lord make myself known to Him in a vision; I speak with him in a dream. **People if your dreams come true, then your duty is to share them for their purpose, not keep them to yourself.**

Don't Be Afraid!

Fight Back -Or- Die for Nothing

My visions God has given me is the best favor that has ever happened to me in this physical world. My dreams have helped me assist people in their walking lives, and there are people that wouldn't dare deny the help of God Himself. *Your gifts are meant to be shared.*

Acts 16:9

And a vision appeared to Paul in the night: and a man of Macedonia was standing there, urging him, and saying, "Come over to Macedonia and help us." *People if you are having visions and clear sight, then use your visions for the greater good.*

"The countless people I've help over the years in my lifetime. Pure strangers, family, neighbors, and friends. My God, what do we do with our gifts?

Use Them for the Greater Good!

Surviving the Enemy

True Event:

I was in yet a tender relationship with "Big Face C" rather handsome in his own way. They were our neighbors on **Pomeroy Rd. SE. DC**. I rather be specific with my encounters for there isn't a single lie in this here power in your hands! While it lasted, I was able to forewarn **C** of a tragedy coming his way. He spent the night at my house, and while sleeping I dreamed some guys tried to rob him, and he fought back causing harm to the robber. In the struggle to rob him they shot him wounding him severely. I awaken in a cold sweat and immediately warned him. Of course, he was upset with me, having such a dream about him. He got dress and left to tend to his little sister and grandmother. I remember a week almost two weeks maybe, going by without seeing him. I wondered if I scared him off, or did, he think I was some freak or something. I saw his Uncle and asked has he seen **C**, and that's when he told me C was in the hospital and had been shot around where he hangout. **Yes,** my heart dropped, and I remember having this outer body experience. His uncle told me what hospital He was in, and of course I went to go see him. **People**, I swear if it wasn't for me waking up with him beside me in a cold sweat from the dreamed I had about him. I believe he would have thought I set him up. **But God Right!** It had saddened me to see him lying there hurt. We shared a few words, I told him "how sorry I was, and I only wanted to help him" and with relief he told me, "it wasn't my fault." I asked him what happened and he told me, *"it happened the way I said it had happened"* two guys tried to rob him, and he was able to fight the dudes off, and the other pulled a gun and shot him. He told me if he'd listen to me, he would've been with me not up there.

Long story short people our gifts are not to be taken lightly especially if you know it is your duty to warn.

Fight Back -Or- Die for Nothing
Truth in the Matter

My aunt **D** would always tell me, **"*Jennifer God has open so many doors for you*"** I never took it into consideration the doors I've been through were opened by God, and the miracles He's planted in my life until my daughter. Over the years of growing and developing into a beautiful confident woman I come to know that God knows exactly how I feel. My every worry, my every tear drop, and even my pain He somehow, someway fixed everything in my favor. The world and the people in it will turn its back on you if they knew you had the favor of God on your life. **Trust me I know!** I lost my family, and even those I have seen as friends when God kept restoring my life. God Kept picking me up whenever I got knocked down. He continued to restore me with the favor of the Holy Spirit to deal with my adversaries whenever they came up against me. **Today,** I know without a doubt, "I am the Daughter of the true living God." A chosen child to do his works in whatever it is He ask of me. The hurt this world has to offer has nothing to do with the power of God when He renews you. ***People,*** know who our God is, and then seal Him in your hearts and never lose faith. Losing faith is where Satan awaits you.

Keeping hope alive in you is your doorway to the power of Jesus Christ our Lord and Savior. Invite Him in and He will cleanse everything about you, and around you. It's a bumpy and uncomfortable road, but it's sure is worth the trip.

Selah…

Surviving the Enemy

Your Birth Right

People this is one of the most important messages in this power you hold in your hands. Our focus is to remain on Jesus, Lord over all things **(Hebrews1:2; Psalm 2:7-8; Mathew28:18)** through His grace and our faith in Him, are counted as joint heirs **(Romans 8:17; Galatians 3:29; Titus 3:7)**. People your birthright is not to be toyed with. Nor should it be stricken from you through treachery, trickery, theft nor murder. People we are continuously warn to steadfast, and not be foolish as Esau who, with hastiness gave away his birthright for a bowl of stew **(Hebrews 12:16-17; Genesis 25:19-34)**. Esau's asinine thinking caused him his birthright and the blessing of his father **(Genesis 27)**. People, there's things you do in this world and then there's things you just don't do in this world! We must honor God, and everything spiritual and holy. This includes whatever your birthright is. Never give up what's important, Godly or honorable for the sake of your flesh-eating pleasures. ***Never!***

Rather you're born first, or last; what is meant for you is for you, and there's nothing no one can do to take that away from you. Our Father the true living God, covered your birth right before you were born. Your birth right has nothing to do with the promise of man, but it has everything to do with the promise of God our Lord and Savior. Don't be the receiver of nothing to fulfill a minute of hunger. ***Don't be the recipient to fulfill and hour of pleasure***. Be the faith that mankind needs, and the hope unseen. ***Pray for everything you need in Christ Jesus where all power and might lays within His people.*** The NKJV Bible shares the birthright of sons, but I'm here to tell you, as the daughters of the King *"**Yee All You Daughter's**" your birthright is there given to you by the law of the Holy Spirits and our true King.*

Fight Back -Or- Die for Nothing

Never turn away from it! Never give it away! Fight for it as it is yours by birthright! Woe to those of you who try to impersonate, steal, rob, and kill for a right that doesn't rightfully belong to you. Heirs are not rumoring, we come by the decade. If you sit on a thrown that doesn't belong to you, the day will come that you will be overthrown by the might of a rightful heir.

So, it is written!

Selah and pray in all truth!

CHAPTER TEN

My Real Father (Finally)

I had a dream of when I was two years old. My only memory of this dream was my feet, and my dad walking side by side together. ***Waking from this dream with whom I assumed was my father tortured me for years.*** In walking life, I was abandoned at two years old by my biological dad. Over the years I wept wondering what was so bad that he would leave me and my mother. To fill the emptiness when I inquired about my dad, my mother and aunt would speak highly of him over the years. Their stories always gave me something to look forward come the day I found him. They shared stories about how he used to shop for me at stores like, "Seventh Heaven" back in the day, and how he used to buy me the prettiest, and most expensive dresses in the store. During that time, they said, "he was good to me and my mother." Always bringing her money and taking her out. Stay with me, I'm going somewhere with this; my mother then realized their outings were either at her house, or in his car.

The Car!

Selah....

Fight Back -Or- Die for Nothing

People, you know where I'm going with this. I was conceived in the drive-in movie theater. In the back seat of my dad's car. My God people, this is a moment to pause, because the Lord Jesus Christ had given a special permission for me to be conceived. ***In the back seat of my father's car though.*** People, God has something to do with every life conceived, and brought into this world. Just as were given our gifts before brought into this world, God knew my dad was married, and seen my mother being the side chick. Yes, my mother was the other women! Did she know this? ***No,*** I could tell from all the anger she harbored over the years against him. My mother was heartbroken to have learned my dad was married. When I was old enough, I searched high and low for him. My aunt DR informed me my dad was well and alive. ***Not dead,*** how they exclaimed to my mother. ***To end my dad's affairs, they told her he was stabbed and killed by his nephew.*** Years later my aunt DR informed me my father could be found gambling in Atlanta City casinos. *"I know where one of my habits derived."* She was going to tell me where I could find him, but sadly she was shot and killed by a stray bullet as she set in her window around **Robinson PL SE. DC.** Call me crazy, but the timing of events is all too impeccable! ***Just impeccable I tell you.*** I didn't give up there, my father was alive out there somewhere. My heart knew after all these years he was alive and well. There was this knowing that lived in me, and lived in my mother that he was still alive. Through a network of feuding princes, led me to a house in **NE. DC.** They received me and made a phone call that was a knock away from my dad. They came back with news, "I wasn't entitled to anything." I was exited in a hurry by an escort, as if a threat was imminent. Outside I was told again, "I wasn't entitled to anything," and they had nothing for me. What they didn't know was, I didn't want anything, except to get to know whom my siblings were, and to hug a guy, my heart yearned so much for over the years. This was the closest I ever came to knowing him. Never giving up on my pursuit for him. People, I had my heart ripped out, yet again, fulfilled with a truth, he wasn't dead Afterall, as **Aunt DR** was sure about.

Surviving the Enemy

Why the denial, why the lies of being murdered? Why the betrayal, and why did he resurface after my mother died? So, many why's? Sometime later the opportunity presented itself to put a face with a name. **That's right people, EJ** showed his face on social media soon after my mother died. So, not only did he fake his death to my mother with the story of his nephew stabbing him, and killing him, but he had also been seen gambling in **Atlanta City**. Just as **Aunt DR** was sure of, not to mention my trip to the social security building requesting his information. Even there I was informed he was entitled to his privacy. Even dead men are entitled to privacy I learned. Who was **EJ, why such a cover-up to hide his iniquities**? I cried to my King to reveal his where about if he was still on this earthly plain. My God does our King have a way with *revelations.* A few weeks after my mother died this man whom I never seen before, stained my heart with a picture I created of him from all the stories told over the years. **People,** when God gives us *revelations,* He makes no mistake. The man I sketched in my head looked exactly like the man whom appeared out the blue on face book, seemingly moments after my mother died.

My body does this thing when God reveals truth, He wants me aware. I had to make sure it was him. I took his picture to my aunt, and uncle and for sure enough my aunt identified him as my father, beside the weight he gained over the years. My aunt's identification was enough for me to call him out! **Behold, he** didn't deny it, but informed me, "he let another man do what he couldn't." He didn't care about what I been through, and didn't care to know who I was. Denying the little girl in me all over again. I made sure to expose him to his family as he was portraying to be an upright Christian. I told my Uncle **B,** his brother, and accepted his children's friend request. My Uncle **B** said **EJ** wasn't going to deny me no further if I was truly his daughter.

Fight Back -Or- Die for Nothing

My Uncle *B*, disturbed by the news, called his brother my dad, and approached him with my allegations, and for the first time in forty years my dad *called me,* and still toyed with me unashamed. I offered a paternity test, blood test, saliva test whatever he needed to put this to rest. *EJ*, promised when he came back from his training with his job, he would give me a call. *People,*

I never received that call.

But My Real Father King Jesus Was Right on Time!

Amen!

Surviving the Enemy

Why Am I Sharing This Now?

A few magnificent reasons, *one* being there are so many of us out here in the world born out of wedlock, or one-night stands, the *back seat in a drive in-movie theater,* and failed relationships. Walking around half empty filling unwanted, stigmatized a bastard child due to an unknown parent or no parents due to unforeseen circumstances. *I'm here to tell you don't give up hold them accountable.* Ask God to assist you in your pursuit for answers, as He can do abundantly all things in light of truth. *People,* God didn't leave us empty hearted and fatherless. God knew my pain and foresaw the hole enlarging in my heart. To temper my yearning, he sent me *VHM* the best dad a girl could've asked for. A father that later gave me and my brother a little sister *SLW.* God then, years later blessed us with a stepdad. Indeed, a blessing in our lives in our later years. I stand by him today until God calls him home. In all we see as abandonment, God has somehow fulfilled what was empty in us, by providing us with not the missing pieces, but pieces to restore our emptiness.

So, thank you *EJ* for letting greater men than you, do what you couldn't do for the little girl you were given permission of our Lord and Savior to create. Thank you for abandoning my mother, because I would've never met the men, *I call my dad(s)*. Out of this adventure I searched high and low for you. I come to learn I was never without my real *Father*, Jesus Christ, and my grandfather *God,* King of all Kings. *I was never alone!* I had a *Father* the day I was thought about, and the day I was born. My Father was there, God was there, and the Holy Spirit was there, all awaiting my arrival in this world created for us to reign. *So, people I say to you today call out to our real Father, the true King your Lord and Savior,* as He is our real Father and will never forsake us to feel lonely ever again. Call out to Him, and I promise you God will fulfill the emptiness no matter what it has claimed over you. *I am not a bastard child!*

Fight Back -Or- Die for Nothing

Call on the King for answers He will respond with ***revelations***. ***Call*** on Him to strengthen you in Him, He will respond with the same power that raise Jesus from the grave. Call on Him people, it is the power of God in me, that wills this here power in your hands. Believe in Him who is greater than anything you can every face in your life. ***Call*** on Him, ***depend*** on him, trust in him, for it is all He ask of us. ***People***, God our Savior is real in us and in the world, who loves us ***unconditionally***. Trust in His love for you, as you are His children, whom He given a powerful identity to dwell in this world He created. ***For just once,*** once people, trust in Him, trust in the unseen, the power that gives you breath, the power that raised Jesus Christ from the tomb, trust in the ***Heavens*** and the Earth. For just once in your God given life give Him your heart, it is all He ask of thee; is to just believe just this once.

Selah.

Surviving the Enemy

There is power written in everything **Christ Jesus.** I'm not an Expert in the Bible, I'm still being taught by God, and I'm a true testimony of His works. ***All you must do is believe,*** and powerful scriptures such as these will find their way into your life just as these below entered my life.

Romans 15:13
May the God of Hope fill you with all joy and peace in believing, so that by the power of the Holy Spirit you may abound.

Acts 16:31
And they say, "Believe in the Lord Jesus, and you will be saved, you and your household."

Hebrews 11:1
Now faith is the assurance of things hoped for, the conviction of things not seen.

Johns 20:31
But these are written so that you may believe that Jesus is the Christ, the Son of God and that by believing you may have life in His name.

Mark 9:24
Immediately the father of the child cried out and said, "I believe; help my unbelief!"

Psalm 28:7
The Lord is my strength and shield; in Him my heart trusts, and I am helped; my heart exults, and with my song I give thanks to Him.

Fight Back -Or- Die for Nothing

John 5:24 Truly, truly, I say to you, whoever hears my word and believes Him who sent me has eternal life. He does not come into judgement but has passed from death to life.

Romans 10:17 So, faith comes from hearing, and hearing through the word of Christ.

Isaiah 40:31 But they who wait for the Lord shall renew their strength; they shall mount up with wings like eagles; they shall run and not be weary; they shall walk and not faint.

Mark 5:36 But overhearing what they said, Jesus said to the ruler of the synagogue, "Do not fear, only believe."

John 3:16 "For God so loved the world, that He gave His only son, that whoever believes in Him should not perish but have eternal life.

Hebrews 11:6 And without faith it is impossible to please Him, for whoever would draw near to God must believe that He exist and that He rewards those who seek him.

John 3:1-36
Now there was a man of pharisees named Nicodemus, a ruler of the Jews. This man came to Jesus by night and said to Him, "Rabbi, we know that you are a teacher come from God, for no one can do these signs that you do unless God is with hm." Jesus answered him, "Truly I say to you, unless one is born again he cannot see the Kingdom of God." Nicodemus said to him "How can a man be born when he is old? Can he enter a second time into his mother's womb and be born?" Jesus answered, "Truly, truly, I say to you, unless one is born of the water and the spirit, he cannot enter the kingdom of God.

Surviving the Enemy

Hebrews 11:1- 40
Now faith is the assurance of things hoped for, the conviction of things not seen. For by it the people of old received their commendations. By Faith we understand that the universe was created by the word of God, so that what is seen was not made from things that are visible. By faith Abel offered God a more acceptable sacrifice than Cain, through which he was commanded as righteous, God commending him by accepting his gifts. And through his faith, though he died, he still speaks. By faith Enoch was taken up so that he should not see death, and he was not found because God had taken him. Now before he was taken, he was commended as having pleased God.

Proverbs 22:4
The reward for humility and fear of the Lord is riches and honor and life.

John 20:29
Jesus said to him, "Have you believed because you have seen me? Bless are those who have not seen me and yet believed."

Psalm 91: 1-16
He who dwells in the shelter of the Highest will abide in the shadow of the Almighty. I will say to the Lord, "My refuge and my fortress, my God, in whom I trust." For He will deliver you from the snare of the fowler and from the deadly pestilence. He will cover you with His pinions and under His wings you will find refuge; His faithfulness is a shield and a buckler. You will not fear the terror of the night, nor the arrow that flies by day.

Romans5:8 But God shows His love for us in that while we were still sinners, Christ died for us.

Fight Back -Or- Die for Nothing

John 1:12
But to all who died receive him, who believed in his name, he gave the right to become children of God.

1 John 5:14-15
And this is the confidence that we have toward him, that if we ask anything according to his will, he hears us. And if we know that he hears us in whatever we ask, we know the requests that we have asked of him.

1 John 4:16
So, we have come to know and to believe the love that God has for us. God is love, and whoever abides in love abides in God, and God abides in him. Amen

Hebrews 11:11
By faith Sarah herself received power to conceive, even when she was past the age, since she considered him faithful who had promised.

Philippians 4:13
I can do all things through Him who strengthens me.

Acts 6:14
For we have heard him say that Jesus of Nazareth will destroy this place and will change the customs that Moses delivered to us."

John 14:27
Peace I leave with you; my peace I give to you. Not as the world gives do, I give to you. Let not your hearts be troubled, neither let them be afraid.

Surviving the Enemy

John 11:40
Jesus said to her, "Did I not tell you that if you believed you would see the glory of God?"

Mark 11:23
Truly, I say to you, whoever says to this mountain, "Be taken up and thrown into the sea; and does not doubt in his heart but believes that what he says will come to pass, it will be done for him.

Daniel 6:23
The King was exceedingly glad, and commanded that Daniel be taken up out of the den. So, Daniel was taken up out of the den, and no kind of harm was found on him, because he had trusted in his God.

Jeremiah 17:5
Thus, says the Lord; "Cursed is the man who trusts in man and makes flesh his strength, whose heart turns away from the Lord.

Fight Back -Or- Die for Nothing

A Note from the Author
JB
Daughter of the King

People, embed these scriptures into your hearts and your walking life as the promise of God, faith will change the way your eyes look upon this world. As God so much loved us, He created an earth for us to seek the fruitful pleasures of this world. God empowered us the Holy Spirit to multiply for His Kingdom. He gifted us the joys of this world to receive His blessings. We must know his bidding for our lives. These scriptures will assist you in your walk with God and your faith in the unseen. Just because you don't see faith, doesn't mean faith isn't at its best.

Selah.

Surviving the Enemy

Dear COVID – 19,

You Really SUCK & That's Putting It Lightly! I want you to know our father is bigger than you and any problem you can throw at His children. An enemy you are that we can't see attacking us taking us out cowardly. I say to you Covid-19, please show your ugly face. Your nothing like faith which is unseen good and full of Gods promises. You've taken life and want us to remember your wrath against this nation, but as God has taught us, tomorrow you will be no more, and we will remember our families. *You tried to make a purpose in our lives to instill fear, but as God has already taught us everything on the other side of you beholds a cure and His continued promises in our lives.* You are nothing more than a delayal in our purpose, and soon about to be no more. God's chosen are now at war with you and the foundation from which you came! Gods army has gotten bigger sooner than expected, yet still working in our favor as you took life that didn't belong to you. Our lost love ones are at work in Heaven waging a Holy weapon to pursue you. *God's chosen are at work here on earth working relentlessly to rid of you with the entire armor of God.* So, continue to toy with God's children, this Human race, and our humanity. You will not continue to take life! I pray and have faith, and hope our bodies not only create an antibody, but we use against you the same weapon you've evaded our space, persons, children, parents, and His promise for our lives. *You FAILED COVID-19!* Our God Is Alive & Crushing You Every Day That His Children Overcome you!

With Joy & Pleasure we plot a cure against you.

JB, Daughter of the King

Fight Back -Or- Die for Nothing

Dear COVID -19 I hope you,

Surviving the Enemy

_____
_____
_____
_____
_____
_____
_____
_____
_____
_____
_____
_____
_____
_____
_____
_____
_____
_____
_____
_____
_____
_____
_____
_____
_____
_____
_____
_____
_____.

P.S. I'm Taking Back the Power You Stole from Me.
Signed_____
_____**!!!**

Fight Back -Or- Die for Nothing

A Little Exposure About Me the Author!

I'm a Summer baby and was raised by women who roared like lions when it came to war battling for what they believed. The women in my family didn't know how not to fight. That I got honestly speaking of, "apples falling straight from the bloodlines and the vines from which I came." I come from a mother who was the sixth child of the seven. I'm the middle child of my mother's three children and come from a sizable family. *Surely*, where you saw one the others followed. That was in love, war, celebrations, reunions, and other personal matters of the heart, even funerals. I knew, in the power of God surely in me, I was different, and I accepted it some years ago. *I wrote this book to help every human being I possibly can.* By sharing my downfalls and the many times God has saved my life. *Especially,* picking me up after being left broken by those I once trusted.

God showed me to trust only Him, as He never instructed me to trust humans with my heart, but was very clear in saying, "trust Him." Every morning I'm allowed another day on this beautiful earth I thank God verbally, and I than see my King, and Thank Him personally by Kissing His hands and Feet. God has relish in me a strength I see as a gift to overcome all that challenges me, and all that plots against His will for my life. *People,* I am proof that God lives, as my life has been saved and renewed numerous times. Today I share this piece of power with you as it is going to bring forth change in your life. God has given me a family, *not perfect,* but I love them despite of the evil in this world. God has maintained my stubbornness, fulfilling my life, and every desire for not minding looking crazy, while believing in my heart He lives. As stubborn as I am, I'm thankful for the women in my family for molding me into the women I am today with the same God leading them.

Surviving the Enemy

Most importantly I'm thankful for a one "Lisa Lee Walker" for after permission was given, you brought me into this world, and loved me all you could've. For that, I am forever thankful for your bests. The Love for my mother conquered all evil from her upbringing and mines. I loved you from a mustard seed, and even now after death. Thank you for checking in on me from time to time and answering me whenever I think of you.

To the women in my family where do I start? **Aunt BW**, Aunt **NG**, **Aunt SDW**, "**Aunt PJW** I Love You Auntie" **Uncle F,** and those that have joined our Father, Lord and Savior Mommy **Lisa Lee Walker** and **RLW.** You all are courageous, powerful, meaningful, and protective in all you've bestowed upon this family. Because of your wits and your ways, I now believe in something much bigger than I could've ever imagine for my life. I know I'm seen as the *lone wolf,* but you should be proud, because it's your fighting ways, mistakes made, and lessons learned over the years, that has taught me strength is unseen, felt, and shown in our mental strength that brings about forces to be reckoned and witnessed. Lord knows the force, that came with the wrecking, for those that came up against us. I guess what I'm trying to say is, "Thank you for loving me, protecting me, fighting for me, and loving me in a world where even you were force to grow-up alone. Thank you for your best. Our bloodline is strong, and it must continue for the bloodline we leave behind where the future awaits them.

Forever Grateful.

JWB.

Fight Back -Or- Die for Nothing

To the Blood Line

Despite our differences the future belongs to our heirs. Just as the women before us paved the way for us, we must pave the way for our heirs to lead this bloodline in the way it needs to survive the future, and our enemies. Our momma's ain't raise no fools! The enemy wants us departed! Departed we fall! In our differences and our steadfast as a unit we stand a greater chance against the enemy! ***Never forget it!*** No one is above God, ***No One!!!***

The Laws has Nothing to do with Spiritual Warfare. Trust God and You Will Have Victory in All Things.

Especially Not Man!

God Is Our Only Sustainer Not Men.

Surviving the Enemy

Dear Daughter,

    A precious gift you are to me. A pain reliever once where my heart was filled with pain and sorrow. Your presence in my life was moored than enough to steadfast against all that plagued me over the years. It was God that new you would be the perfect remedy to heal my heart. It was our Lord and Savior whom saideth, I was fit to not just love you, but saw me fit to be your mother. He foresaw the threats against our path, and foresaw me fit to protect you along this rocky road, to love you and raise you as my own. Against the masses I stood, and against the masses I still stand in the fight for you. Over the years I wonder why He chose me, as I was just a child myself, unknowingly being molded for His glory, and His Kingdom to lead many. My strength is a power I couldn't handle in my younger years, but now I know it's true application. It is the same strength now embedded in you from me and God. My child, daughter of Jennifer Lee Walker Brown, and Granddaughter of Lisa Lee Walker you are the heir of our strength, and a Walker by the right of God! Never let no one tell you different! Your ties to me doesn't come from my bloodline but from God. You're tied to me by a power greater than blood, by the same power that raised Jesus from the grave, and by the same power that gives us breath in every second of our day. At three weeks old by the power invested by God in us made you mine with no legal authority involve, and by the power that covers us you are still my daughter. No weapon on this earth will ever change that in life nor in death.

That I Pray & Selah!

JB,

Your Mother & Daughter of the King.

Fight Back -Or- Die for Nothing

Acknowledgements

Dear People,

God places feudal princes, feminism, and libertarians in our wake intentionally. To the human eye this occurs by pure coincidence. People, do yourselves Godly favor and start paying attention to spiritual warfare, because nothing happens by pure coincidence. God knows exactly what he's doing. If the Lord orders our paths to cross, make no second thought about it. If it's the plot of Satan's aim on your life, make no mistake under God's covenant He will intervene. People, the enemy only wins if you give in to the tools developed to destroy you. Only you know your weakness.

Only You!

JB, *Daughter of the King.*

Extra Thanks & Acknowledgements

To Prayer Teams Known and Unknown! Thank you for praying me and my family through during our darkest hours. I would not have sustained without your individual prayers for my life and my families. I want you to know I felt every prayer

through strength, adaptivity, and power I didn't know I had in me to fight. You are the miracles at work on this earth. You are the light in dark places. Your prayer impacted the power I thought was extinguished. Your prayers and your will for my life and my family have pulled us through. You should be proud of the power that resides in you, because you all gave me a second wind. I thank God for you I love you and just know that we were aware of you rooting and praying for us.

Fight Back -Or- Die for Nothing

*I*n the darkness the enemy forces you to hide. *I* think it's time to shed a little light on the enemy. *W*hat do you say prayer team*?* *T*ogether we stand; *T*ogether the enemy will succumb. *I* don't mind lighting the torch!

JB – *Daughter of the King/Creator & Author*

JB, is the author of Surviving the Enemy and appreciates you holding this powerful tool in your hands! She's not just an author, she is a survivor too! JB bestow a spiritual belief that's unwavering! JB, originated from Washington, DC., born and raise. She now resides in Maryland with her family. She received a Bachelor of Science in Criminal Justice Studies in 2011. JB hopes, Surviving the Enemy is as inspiring, as it was powerful in her overcoming countless attacks of the enemy. Now, a powerful tool for the generations to come. JB, is passionate about the human purpose and hopes Surviving the Enemy helps you find yours.

Fear Is Not an Option, But A Task – Conquer It.

2nd Timothy 1:7 For God has not given us a Spirit of fear, but of Power and of Love and Sound Mind.

I've Been Taught Well – *JB.*

Fight Back -Or- Die for Nothing

*D*ear *G*od,

Thank you for giving me the strength to step outside of the fear the enemy set fire around me! Why they all hate me so much I'll never know, but your love for me is so much greater than the enemy's hate and sabotage on my life. Thank you for giving me the strength and methodology to fight the false accusations, and cases that came up against me from state to state. Thank you for giving me grace when the enemy enforced wreckage and havoc in my life. Thank you for giving me discernment and allowing me to tap into the gifts given to me at birth! Thank you for choosing me to withstand the wilds of the enemy, as you foresaw everything before I could comprehend the enemy's reason for choosing me. Thank you for trusting me to overcome all these task and challenges with you leading me. My Life as I Know It Has No Purpose Without You!

Sincerely,

Your Daughter JB...

Exposing the Enemy
Coming Soon!

*You Have A Choice!
Death
Isn't an Option
Before Your Purpose Is
Fulfilled.*

Surviving the Enemy

Certificate of Registration

This Certificate issued under the seal of the Copyright Office in accordance with title 17, *United States Code,* attests that registration has been made for the work identified below. The information on this certificate page has been made part of the Copyright Office records.

Registration Number
TXu 2-122-118
Effective Date of Registration: October 26, 2018

Title of Work:
Surviving the Enemy

Completion Publication Year:
2018

Copyright Claimant: Jennifer L. Brown
Citizen of: United States
Domiciled in: United States Author
Created: Text
Author: Jennifer L. Brown
New Material Included in Claim: Text

Fight Back -Or- Die for Nothing

Contact JB, for More Information on Overcoming the Enemy

<u>*SURVIVINGTHEENEMY2020@AOL.COM*</u>

IT'S NEVER TOO LATE!